*for Brenda Watson,
with regards,
Ralph Ruddock.
August '95*

Democracy and Learning

Ralph Ruddock

Manchester Monographs
The centre for adult and higher education.
University of Manchester

© R. Ruddock

October 1994

ISBN 0 902252 25 9

Printed by

GMCVS Print Service
St Thomas Centre, Ardwick Green North, Manchester M12 6FZ.
Tel: 0161-273 5869.

ACKNOWLEDGEMENTS

My thanks to Brian Nichol and Mike Davis for collegial advice and support; to David Solomon for current perspectives on Kibbutz; to Eileen Clarke for extensive editorial revision and improvements to my original draft; to Sherri Crampton for the typing of a difficult text.

Thanks also to the following for permission to quote from their publications:

The Bertrand Russell Foundation: M. Raptis, **Self Management in the struggle for Socialism.**

United Nations Research Institute for Social Development: A. Pearse and Matthias Stiefel, **Inquiry into Participation, 1979.**

Thames and Hudson Ltd: P. Green, **A Concise History of Ancient Greece.**

Religious Society of Friends, Philadelphia: M. Sheeran, **Beyond Majority Rule.**

Freedom Press: Ward, C. **Introduction to Fields, Factories, Workshops.**

The Observer: P. Thompson, 29.1.89.

The Guardian: The Seikatsu Club. 1988.

Dr Margaret Ledwith, for use of the network diagram on p xx (Chapter 10 p2)

CONTENTS

Introduction		1
Chapter One	On Feeling Sick at Election Time	3
Chapter Two	The Crisis of the Israeli Kibbutz	12
Chapter Three	Classical Athens: the Supreme Instance	19
Chapter Four	Quakers: Three Hundred Years without a Leader	42
Chapter Five	Self-Government in Industry and Trade	54
Chapter Six	Co-operatives	68
Chapter Seven	Collective Responsibility, Learning and the Quality of Life	78
Chapter Eight	Anarchism: theory and practice	92
Chapter Nine	The Microcosm: Leaderless Groups	100
Chapter Ten	Possibilities and Resistances	109
Bibliography		129

Introduction

> *Your British subject, the Greek (of Periclean Athens) might say, as soon as he has elected his Member of Parliament, has abdicated. He has no more to say in international questions; even in his own city, he does not count, when once he has elected a Town Council. As a result, the Greek would go on to say, he loses interest in half of the things that really make him a man; he leaves it to Parliament to frame the laws; to the King or the prime minister to decide on war and peace; to the judges to decide cases in the law courts; to old aldermen to arrange market dues and street cleaning and the height of buildings. What has the Englishman left for him to do? The Englishman's life, according to the Greek, is the merest broken arc of the full circle of man's life, and the Englishman, as a result, ends by being a mere decimal of a man, a vulgar fraction, a negation of nature. Yes, there is something unnatural, the Greeks would say, about this whole scheme of delegating powers; you English are barbarians; you are not really free, but subjects; hence your undeveloped, yes! your atrophied minds.*
>
> T.R. Glover, 1935. St. Johns, Cambridge

The above condenses the main argument of this text. Relying on the work of specialist scholars, it presents evidence from seven fields, sufficient, it is hoped, to demonstrate its validity. Self-government is seen as the alternative to the conservative, socialist and reform ideologies at present on offer, but it does not yet know itself to be the alternative. The purpose here is to promote self-knowledge, with some reference to self-formation in the participatory experience. The final chapters examine some of the implications and problems of implementation, and the sources of predictable opposition. The British are the most sceptical people in the Western World. They have had reason enough.

A sense of revulsion at election time is general. Yet most people are willing to vote, not so much, perhaps, because they are convinced by what is on offer, or have faith that a given party will honour its promises; but rather because they wish to affirm their adherence to some general values, and especially to exclude a party they conceive of as the enemy. An increasing number are disenchanted with the process; they vote with their feet at elections times and occupy themselves with something they find more worthwhile. Or they may vote in the spirit of a French lady at their last presidential election. She was faced with two unappetising candidates and, while conceding that one of them was offering policies that could be of value (if the offer were genuine and feasible) said, *"I suppose I'll have to get drugged up and vote for him."*

But the general dissatisfaction is deeper than a concern for personalities, or even for their probity. The party system we have, claiming to be representative, is, in fact, so unrepresentative of the infinite range of individual opinion on the wide range of specific issues, that the citizen becomes invisible. He is lost in the mass, and is seen as *"one million divided by a million"*, in Koestler's phrase.

Yet all citizens have a life-time of experience. As mature men and women, they have formed considerable opinions on many issues that call for decision. Usually, they are willing to acknowledge their ignorance on others that have lain outside their experience. They will insist that they have formed their own views, and are not reflecting those propagated by the media. In this, they may be deceiving themselves: better informed, they would form better judgements. Their responses, however, their thought processes, and especially their experience, should be respected. They should not be massified and obliterated, as in our present non- representative democracy. There are alternatives: this text presents chapter-length accounts of some of them. But we first need to identify some of the deficiencies and deceptions inherent in the present system.

Chapter One

On Feeling Sick at Election Time

The constituency in which you live may have returned a member of the same party over several elections. The majority may have been of the order of three to one, perhaps even four to one. Some swing of opinion is possible; a 15% swing has been recorded in your constituency, and in the polls, but your local result would only be affected in case of a 30% swing, which is unlikely to happen. Therefore, you conclude, there is not the slightest point in your voting, or taking any account of the election. A friend will, no doubt, say: *"Yes, but if everybody ..."*: to whom you recommend a study of the theory of probability.

Your decision not to vote is certainly rational, and it may be the only rational one, in fact. You are, however, bombarded by post, radio and television with appeals and arguments. You are put under pressure to act, to speak, to think, as if your vote made any difference. As a child, you may have enjoyed *Charades*. Even now, you might be willing, occasionally, to play some political simulation game as a pastime. To be asked to join such a game on the pretext that what you do will be of some consequence, and to find that other participants apparently take it for real, might, at the start, cause you to feel queasy; on their account, perhaps.

But suppose the case is different. If it is known that in your constituency opinion is balanced and the outcome uncertain, will not voting then be valid? Up to a point, perhaps; but you may find that other aspects of the electoral process press upon you, and your nausea rises again. Even a superficial diagnosis will identify a great deal of what is being fed to you as being difficult to swallow, impossible to digest.

Some such items are summarily listed below:

1. You are insulted by the insistent appeal to self-interest. As you belong to the fairly comfortable majority, you are concerned rather for the third world; and for the recently doubled numbers of our own population living below the poverty line, or homeless; or the many discharged ex-

patients from psychiatric institutions exposed to the absence of community care; and the long-term unemployed and their families. All of these are rated third, fourth or fifth on party programmes.

2. You observe that the party which ruled Britain throughout the 1980s was elected on a minority vote, and was able to carry through radical right-wing policies against the weight of public opinion. You observe that two million Greens emerge from an election with no parliamentary representatives. You ask yourself whether it can ever be right to participate in such a skewed system.

3. You observe that against something over £8 million gathered by the left for a recent election campaign, the right had more than eight million pounds, plus many large, hidden subventions, and an ever-ready willingness, as it would seem, on the part of your favourite retailers, such as Sainsbury's and Marks & Spencer, to provide more, if it should appear to be necessary. Martin Linton published in January, 1994 his research findings into the preponderance of right-wing publicity freely given by newspapers during the last election. He calculated its value using a sophisticated American formula which differentially rated selected news items, editorial coverage and advertising space, on a points basis. *The Express, The Mail* and *The Sun* scored an aggregate 1,773 points favourable to the conservatives, with an additional 3,175 points unfavourable to Labour, a total bias of 4,948 points. Only *The Mirror* presented a reverse bias of 1,406 points. Neutral items totalled 2,060, distributed between the four newspapers and the three main parties. The commercial value of this newspaper space, duly rated, was estimated at almost £60 million, tabloids accounting for £37 million. (**Money and Votes**. Martin Linton. IPPR, London.)

The Daily Mirror has since abandoned its support for the Labour cause; the Conservatives, may, therefore, be expecting the propaganda power of the popular press to maintain them in office for decades.

Britain and Japan are the only large countries which do not regulate newspaper reporting at election time in accordance with some proportionate principle.

There are pseudo-democracies around the world. If, as in Burma, Nigeria and Angola, they allow a genuine expression of popular preference and then suppress it by military means, the situation is clear for all to see. In more sophisticated countries, a similar result may be obtained by the agency of the media, rather than the military — Britain is heading in that direction.

4. You then recall that, from 1979, when the right hired the services of a great advertising agency to spearhead its propaganda drive, others have followed suit. You ponder the political implications of elections as a war of the agencies.

5. You become more sharply aware that between 80% and 90% of the popular press is in the hands of right-wing autocrats; that the autonomy of the BBC has been severely compromised by imposed financial stringency, and by the intimidation in respect of the licence fee: also by enforced debasement of standards, in order to boost viewing figures; that there is still no right of reply or adequate means of redress against media abuse. In the face of such one-dimensional orientation of image, persuasion and selective data, you ask yourself how it can be possible for voters to think politically. You question whether you are, yourself, able to do so; even to stand still amid the torrent let alone to swim against it.

6. Perhaps you listen to a T.V. debate between matched political opponents. You quickly reach two conclusions.

a) A debate is a hopeless method of reaching a considered view on any question;

b) The opponents know each other quite well. They have met before, and learned each others' arguments, even to the letter. You realise it would be perfectly possible for them to exchange roles, and to recite each other's sentences, even with the indignation that may seem appropriate. What kind of debate is this?

7. Sometimes, one is able to observe a politician whose responsibilities have been changed at short notice. It could be a move from a responsibility in the Health Service to a senior post in the Foreign Office. Three days later, he is presented on television and complex questions relating to Africa or the Middle East are put to him. He then plays his part as an instant expert on the world.

You may even be impressed. He has "learned his lines". Government policies on all issues have been pre-formulated, and every politician has learned to respond to questions by repeating his party's formula; or by taking the opportunity to expand on a different issue.

8. And what of the grooming? Every lock of hair, real or otherwise, must be gelled into place. A suitable complexion must be provided. After all,

who wants a pallid foreign secretary? And then, style. *"Train yourself to appear sincere and genuine"*, advises the renowned Michael Shea in his book on Influence; and Laurence Olivier, asked for the secret of his success as an actor: *"Sincerity, sincerity. Once you fake that, you can achieve anything."*

According to Dr Kissinger, speaking in a BBC programme on the making of a presidential successor to Ronald Reagan, a prospective candidate must have the following characteristics:

a) He must be an ego-maniac;

b) He must have a substantial private income;

c) He must have contacts and influence enough to be able to raise $15 million quickly in $1,000 bills;

d) He must devote the three years before the election exclusively to the task of winning, spotlighted in monstrous meetings, conferences and conventions.

e) He must be able to speak (and, therefore, to think, one assumes) in the simplest terms, and to adjust his public persona at every indication of grass-roots approval or disapproval. After this, according to Dr Kissinger, if elected, he must start to learn about the current predicaments and policies of the government he will lead, in a great world of which he may know little. The right to elect such a president by mass vote is presented to Americans as a most precious right for which they should be willing to die; and, unfortunately, to kill their neighbours who do not share this vision.

9. If this is not your first election, you will already have learned that the record of a party in power bears little relationship to the programme on which it was elected. The performance of the 1980s Conservative government in relation to interest rates, the balance of payments, inflation, reduction of the civil services, industrial expansion, international competition and unemployment, demonstrates this; as also the 1970s record of the Labour government in relation to South Africa and to nuclear disarmament. So, you may ask, what is the point of voting on a programme? Some voters never do, of course. They vote for people who impress them. Hence the grooming.

You will be well aware that many of the issues that cause you most concern cannot be placed on a left-right spectrum. Many escape from the party lines. These may include:

>   Foreign policy — a range of items.
>   Nuclear disarmament.
>   Proportional representation.
>   National sovereignty.
>   Ecology — again, a range of items.
>   Aid to the third world.
>   Transport policy.
>   Planning generally.
>   Action against Iraq or Serbia.
>   Immigration controls.
>   Media issues; ownership; control; BBC.
>   Sex issues: abortion; pornography; gay rights.
>   Civil liberties.
>   Reforms: judiciary; prisons; police.
>   Equal opportunities; women; minorities.
>   Support for arts; museums; sports.
>   Race relations; fundamentalism.

The list of single-issue concerns could be greatly extended. They are matters about which the majority of voters feel a strong concern — selectively, of course. They do not lend themselves to left/right polarisation. The citizen will, therefore, feel unrepresented. He will find the suggestion that he could be represented by a single political figure, over four years, in a time of rapid change, quite grotesque.

You may find that nausea converts to a subdued rage. You find yourself impelled towards three conclusions:

First, you are perplexed by the fact that millions of apparently rational citizens are prepared to accept such a system, and even participate in it.

Second, finding that there is no-one to represent you, it becomes clear that no-one can ever represent anyone else.

Third, you are forced to conclude that in the name of democracy, the system is purposively structured to exclude the possibility of it: perhaps, you may think, because our rulers feel they have more than enough problems to work through as things are, and it would become intolerable to them if they were required to take into consideration the views of the people on all matters.

It is the purpose of this text to argue that there is an alternative; that opinion and participation on many issues of which you have knowledge or experience could be invited and built into management, administration and government. Rather, we should say, there is an infinity of alternatives; not one prescribed form. Each chapter presents one or more examples where democracy has been valid.

Endemic Corruption in the Casino Economy

In recent years, probably the most famous names in commerce and finance on the British scene have been Maxwell, Nadir, Fayed, Saunders, Ronson and Ratner: all have been central figures in complex stories of fraudulent dealing, on a vast scale. Even their histories are eclipsed by the exploitative operations of the BCCI and of Lloyds itself. Insider dealing on the stock market is out of control. And perhaps most insidious has been the willingness of professional accountants, in large firms and small, to endorse fraudulent financial statements — again, on a vast scale. In Italy, Latin America and the United States, all countries where the drug trade, the Mafia or Triads have penetrated, or arms-trading in the Middle East, the sums, diverted to private gain, exceed the national incomes of some of the smaller states involved. Computer based crime in the UK is estimated at £500 million a year, and cheque card fraud at £1.5 billions. Sir Robert Mark, reflecting on his experience as Commissioner of the Metropolitan Police is said to have defined an honest police force as one that catches more criminals than it employs. One of our bishops has recently said that the economy is out of control — hardly surprising when the intention has been to let it run free. The consequences are still largely unexamined. But now that we see six recent cabinet ministers appointed to the boards, even the chairmanship, of newly privatised industries, with personal share opportunities worth up to £1 million, we may think universal free enterprise was not so much a matter of principle as of self-interest. Everyone is familiar with Lord Acton's observation that power tends to corrupt, and that absolute power corrupts absolutely; not everyone remembers that he went so far as to add: *"Great men are always bad men."* That is indeed the opposite of what was generally supposed to be the case in his generation a hundred years ago, and the tendency is still towards the opposite on the part of some biographers.

De Tocqueville felt that, at time of great collective anxiety, only a *"madman"*, i.e. a public personality with marked psychotic characteristics, can provide the leadership a nation or party needs. His awareness of this is a striking anticipation of the observations of group work pioneers a century later. In our own time the phenomenon continues to manifest itself. The conduct of Nicholai and Elena Ceausescu in the years before their execution was generally condemned in simple moral terms. It would be better to attempt an understanding in long-established psychiatric categories: delusions of grandeur; folie a deux; kleptomania. The recently coined kleptocracy is a useful term, extending the psychiatric concept into political discourse. There have been enough examples of kleptocrats: Ferdinand and Imelda Marcos; Mobutu of Zaire; Bokassa of Chad. It seems that at a certain point in the acquisition of power and possessions, such people have taken off into a world of omnipotent fantasies. Systems of government have played into this pathology. It is the system that we must call into question. A powerfully argued statement of this case from the anarchist position is to be found in Alex Comfort's **Authority and Delinquency in the Modern State,** Routledge, 1950.

Towards an Alternative

The trend towards centralised authoritarian regimes in our time gives rise to its opposite: a grass-roots growth of self-managed initiatives. These are much less visible than the arms of government. Most of them are small-scale, but not all, and it seems that many are growing in size and strength. Most are commercial enterprises, such as producer co-operatives, whilst others are responses to social needs, such as housing associations, credit unions and parent groups. A minority of these declare a political orientation. Their ideological status is generally ambiguous. They may appear as a new wave of capitalist enterprise, based on the worker-shareholder model. Equally, they may be taken as anticipations of the long-predicted revolt of the workers against owners and their managers. In many instances, worker co-operatives have shown themselves to be more efficient, more profitable and more committed than the managements they have supplanted. But as yet, neither capitalist governments, socialist parties nor trades unions have pronounced upon them. They are not characterised as far left or as new right. They seem to be off the political map. One prediction is that their further proliferation, and their independence, will be unwelcome to governments of the right and of the left.

The fact that they can succeed, and can survive in a harsh economic climate, both in commercial enterprise and in social provision, is surely significant. Their existence, in one form or another over many generations, is a manifestation of a fundamental possibility in social organisation, an alternative to the impenetrable and unaccountable hierarchies of bureaucracy in government, and arbitrary management in industry.

Self-managing religious groups, encounter groups, support groups for a wide range of people suffering from disabilities and distresses, innovative communes based on subsistence agriculture, workshops for artist-craftsmen — the list could be greatly extended — all see themselves as making important and necessary provision that the state and the great systems cannot or will not offer. Often enough, it has been the direct experience of those who promote such groups that state- provided training, or welfare, or psychiatry, or finance, or advice, simply do not make contact with what they know to be their own needs, or with what they have to offer.

Contemporary developments have led us to become more aware than our forbears of the difficulties of implementing self-management programmes, arising from two sources. First, the internal problems of structure, process and commitment, Second, the external problems created by always doubtful and generally hostile governmental and economic institutions. The individual and social values manifested in self-management do not generally prevail against the centralism of international finance capital and its expression in national governments. The marginalisation of man is greatly accelerated in our day by the electronic machine. The global machine has no need of most of the world's inhabitants; its need of them becomes less, decade by decade. A Russian economist has estimated world unemployment at 750 millions — one third of the employable population.

It may be that when self-management has proved itself in economic and human terms, it will simply be prevented from developing further. This consideration will help us to moderate any excessive hopes.

The present intention is to bring together instances of participatory practice not usually connected up in our thinking. Each of the instances is well-known and has given rise to a considerable literature in its own right and to specialist scholarship. Accounts of them in this monograph will necessarily be skeletal but with added emphasis where the main principle is felt to have been exemplified. The aim is to develop an argument rather than to write an outline history.

Representative government is manifestly incapable of eliminating corruption. On the contrary, it appears to facilitate it. It is a soft system, too easily penetrated and manipulated in the interests of the rich and powerful. How far such morbid phenomena might be eliminated by the adoption of participative collective responsibility can never be known.

We would be entitled to have high hopes of it, however. This is because the total transparency, the openness to informed questioning, would surely expose corruption.

The following chapters present instances where such questioning has been valid.

Chapter Two

The Crisis of the Israeli Kibbutz

Kibbutz: Expansion and Crisis

The oldest of the Israeli kibbutzim has been in existence since 1910, 35 years before the state of Israel existed. The following table shows the increase in numbers and of individual membership since that time. It is well to bear in mind that the overall influence of the kibbutzim, both in Israel and internationally, has been far greater than one might suppose from the small percentage of their numbers within the total population of Israel, i.e. 2.6% by 1993.

Year	number	members
1920	12	805
1930	29	3,900
1940	82	26,550
1950	214	67,550
1960	229	77,950
1970	229	85,100
1980	255	111,200
1988	270	126,100
1989	270	124,900
1990	270	125,100
1991	270	129,300

(Central Bureau of Statistics, Israel).

From the start, they accepted a pioneering role. By bringing a sophisticated understanding and small-scale technology into effect, they succeeded in making the desert bloom. Water management was fundamental and once achieved, food, fruit and flowers were produced in abundance.

The group psychology of the kibbutz was basically different from that of the producers' co-operative in an industrial society. Commitment to principle was subject to an absolute test from the moment of tented occupation of uncultivated land. Everything was to be done; everything done was visibly reflected in the well-being of the community. The breaking of the land; the planting and care of crops; the construction of buildings for produce, for collective necessities, for communal dormitories and dining rooms and, later, apartments for families, were all tasks that generated the maximum of motivation and mutual regulation.

Kibbutzim, founded in successive decades, passed through well recognised phases. The first explicitly pioneering phase made great physical and social demands on its members. Their subsistence was, necessarily, supplied, but at a basic level. Skills were at a premium; adult learning became a major concern, starting with Hebrew in many cases. During this first phase, each kibbutz worked out its own system of self-government. Collective responsibility, expressed in direct collective decision-making, was common to all. As with all such enterprises, there were internal conflicts of interest and opinion, sometimes passionate. This may be seen as universal, and appropriate.

The second phase was one of consolidation and modest material gain. Economic independence was achieved and some surpluses were available for disposal. These were generally applied to increase of physical capital, the buildings and plant, and to improved amenities in the accommodation. All that had been learned, together with increased capital resources, led to further gains in productivity.

The third phase was characterised by relative prosperity and diversification. The kibbutz model proved to be valid for small-scale industrial production. Standards of commercial and marketing practice were raised, as were educational standards in their small schools. It was partly an outcome of these developments that the principles of the kibbutz system were exposed to severe stresses, which have been totally destructive in some cases.

Religious fundamentalism has been a divisive factor. There has been passionate argumentation between orthodox socialist groups and the non-religious Mapam wing about the keeping of pigs. Variations in role expectations of women in relation to men, and to their children, were issues of deep significance, but have not threatened the basic principle. The rising wealth of most kibbutzim has, however, accelerated the privatisation of family life, in which ownership of television receivers, cars and telephones has been significant. Varying modes of relating to the national economy, expressed in such practices as the use of hired labour and of finance capital, do threaten it, because they carry a risk for the autonomy of the kibbutz.

Kibbutzim have presented to the world, as under a spot-light, the paradigm of the very best qualities to be found in all that is Jewish. However, the basic concept of a residential commune, from which the kibbutz movement took its inspiration, is not Jewish, but European in origin, ultimately, perhaps, Anglo-Saxon. It does not express Jewish fundamentalism, although there are attempts to constrain some kibbutzim to base every decision and every item of practice upon the Torah and the Talmud. This has always proved to be difficult. The essence of the kibbutz, and its appeal, may well derive from its cosmopolitan origins and its universalism.

The general character of the models that arose has to be understood in relation to the dominant ideologies: Zionist/Jewish nationalism, influenced by Zionist socialist thinkers and writers (Borochov and others). The idea of an agricultural communal entity was a direct socialist response to the petty bourgeois trading and family life of the Jews in Eastern Europe. It was an ideal which flourished and maintained its character over the decades but at the present time is necessarily adapting to social, economic and military exigencies. Herbert Spencer defined life as the adjustment of internal relations to external relations — which may involve a struggle to maintain identity. A refusal or an inability to adjust spells death. In fact, several kibbutzim have closed in recent years.

The latent conflict between communal and individual interests became evident in the demands of couples for more private accommodation; to have their children with them; to be wholly responsible for raising their young children rather than surrender them to the collective nursery for most of their free time, as well as working hours. This frequently became a majority demand, so that private family life predominated in kibbutzim prosperous enough to provide the accommodation. The individualistic orientation came to prevail among the young people, especially the more able ones who wished to enter a university. The kibbutzim had always supported such aspirations for a limited number but the expansion of higher education in many fields offered more opportunities than the kibbutzim could match and, for those not destined for the higher learning, travel and television were opening up the vivid scenes of urban life. As always, it proved in the event to be destructive for many of these to whom it was an irresistible temptation.

In Israel, two further external factors have posed serious problems for the kibbutzim. These were the national military needs and the burgeoning industrialisation associated with those needs. It is obvious that, if defence requirements remove the young adults of both sexes for three years of military service, the effect on the collective life of the kibbutz will be disruptive. Furthermore, because of their hardihood and dedication to group needs, the young kibbutzniks were found to be very well fitted for front-line duties. The casualty rate was heavy for some of the kibbutzim. And beyond this, there was the inevitable assimilation to the values of the urban youth, who constituted the bulk of the conscripts. Ultimately, the most insidious influence (though many think of it as liberating) was the industrial, commercial and professional methods at the legal base of urban life. Insofar as this is an individualistic and money-minded culture, it stands in direct contradiction to the values of the kibbutz. It was perhaps, inevitable that tens of thousand of members, of all ages, should seek to escape from the constraints and sometimes the austerities of the kibbutz life by embracing the relative freedom, the opportunities and the spending power of the urban alternative. The urban scene has, after all, been projected hour by hour on the kibbutz television screens throughout the last thirty years. Even a very small urban apartment can offer the deep satisfaction of private property. The possibility of car ownership is a further attraction. And, for the important minority who have been able to display their abilities in the competition for higher education, there is the promise of a more privileged professional life in medicine, the law, higher management or whatever. The kibbutzim have long recognised these developments and many have sought to provide for greater individual ownership and external technical or professional employment, but with no more than partial success.

Two fundamental questions remain. First, after several years, how do the ex-kibbutzniks rate their urban lives as contrasted with their former existence? This question would warrant large-scale survey enquiry to provide some answers. The responses would vary with respect to occupation, age, fortune, sex and individuality. There is anecdotal evidence of a general recognition of the higher quality of the kibbutz life in human terms, but without a corresponding wish to return to it.

The second question arises out of the first. It asks whether the kibbutz will prove to be compatible with the future of Israeli society which, given a measure of stability, is sure to be increasingly technocratic, capitalised and centralised. This is the ultimate question for all communes and co-operatives. All independent grass-roots participative bodies necessarily come into conflict with central governments which, by legal and financial measures, can threaten their survival. In recognising this, we may place responsibility on governments and blame them for extinguishing the promise of a more humane order in society. This view, however, naively assumes that governments have total autonomy. The facts, well enough known, are that all governments, even the most powerful, are inextricably locked into complex international economic relationships, which expose them to a variety of sanctions if they step out of line. Trade barriers, restriction in imports and exports, the withdrawal of capital, currency exchange value, the transfer of manufacturing bases to other countries, the availability of loans for development, credit-rating, the cost of borrowing, harsh terms for repayment, the terms of trade in the commodity markets, the availability of developments in technology or barriers to the purchase of advanced equipment can jeopardise the very survival of an independent economy. Small communes may be allowed to exist and even to prosper, because their scale of operation is of little consequence from the perspective of a minister of finance. If, however, they choose to mount a challenge to the prevailing system, their gesture might seem akin to throwing snowballs into a furnace.

> "Yes — an honest experiment but fraught with the contradictions of nationalism and exclusivism. They are now very much seen as communities whose riches benefit their elite membership. Some think of them as enterprises that only succeeded on the borders of their nation."
> (David M. Solomon, to whom this writer is indebted for comments and information).

Current Anxieties

Contributors to **Kibbutz Trends** and **Kibbutz Studies**, and indirectly to the Internal Communal Studies Association reflect a deepening concern with survival of kibbutz as a value-based commune based on sharing and mutual responsibility. The penetration of the competitive commercial ethos manifests itself increasingly in payment for work, no longer equal; in more members taking outside employment; in more workers hired from outside by kibbutz industry; in more young people leaving their kibbutz, though this tendency is now somewhat abated. There is also an increase in delegation of authority to managerial boards, sometimes supplanting the general assembly, which from the start was the great instrument of their direct democracy.

The greatest danger may prove to be debts amounting to $4 billion, the results of intemperate management decisions to invest in industrial plant at a time when the kibbutzim were well in advance of their competitors. Financial disaster for Israel as a whole and the kibbutzim in particular resulted from gross governmental mismanagement during the Likud era of Menahem Begin and Itzak Shamir. Debts on such a scale could well bankrupt a large proportion of erstwhile prosperous kibbutzim.

Some have concluded that kibbutzim might survive until 2000, but that by 2010 their communal character, social reciprocity and original principles will have been extinguished. There are many historical instances in which value-based communes have been commercially successful, evolving into prosperous companies with no apparent relation to their founders' aspirations. There is however no trend towards the establishment of urban kibbutzim.

Historically, the kibbutz has been the most successful commune. Survival exigencies gave rise to the basic motivation to succeed, from the moment of foundation. Commitment, the acceptance of a communal ethic, was the key factor.

There remains a general testimony to the personal qualities of kibbutzniks. They are the prime example of the formation of personality within a self-governing system. There is some hope that their strength and realism will bring about a new mode of accommodation with a world of trans-national capitalism, which is abysmally failing to meet the most basic needs of the majority of mankind.

Overall, the kibbutz movement has thrown a brilliant light on one set of social possibilities, and has aroused world-wide interest. Its influence has been far greater than might be expected from their membership, which constitutes no more than 2.6% of the population of Israel. Especially impressive has been the general testimony to the quality of the citizens who have been formed in them from childhood, to the quality of life and the satisfaction expressed by life-time members. This stands in contrast to the many accounts of the miserable collapse of so many utopian socialist communities over the generations. Not all such attempts have failed; but to demand integration of the collective economy with collective life comes near to seeking a solution for the problems of social life in general. Whatever their destiny over the next decades, the example of the kibbutzim remains. They have demonstrated one way to square the circle of social and individual self-interest.

The Communal Life

Some of the most problematic issues in communal life are highlighted by Allen Butcher, writing in the Bulletin of the International Communal Studies Association. He endorses the view of the Association's Director, Donald Pitzer, of the need to study the factors that led to the establishment of a commune, and those which led to its eventual dissolution, as well as the inner processes during its existence.

This involves analysing the commune's relations with the social system which forms its context. It is relevant, for the argument of the present text, which foresees centralised nation-states as likely to crush, or simply erode by taxation, military exigencies, economic policies, co-operative and communal developments when they eventually prove themselves and increase in numbers.

Butcher observes that communalism is *"the Medium, not the Message; almost any ideal may be served by it: religious or secular, pacifist or violent, authoritarian or participatory, ethical or detestable."* This calls for especial emphasis in our time, when the power of militant fundamentalism becomes increasingly dangerous. The intensification of social bonds engendered by communal living offers the perfect means for sects, and even great religions, to mount their assault on civic society. The only value system that cannot form a base for communal living is that of competitive materialism. Butcher sees communalism as the only alternative to that. That is a very large statement, and one not easy to refute.

He sees communal systems as managing production, distribution and consumption by direct human contact, without the use of a monetary system. There is enough evidence to allow the claim that the non- monetary system serves human needs better, and is experienced as more satisfying. He recognises that welfare and education provision in capitalist systems are not based on monetary exchange values. This is also the case with the military. Butcher notes the irony *"that capitalism relies on a form of communalism to protect itself."* This is very real. It has been a commonplace of post-war society that old soldiers, tough characters one might expect, prove to be astonishingly, even emotionally, sentimental about the comradeship they experienced in war. To find the moral equivalent of that has been recognised as the great challenge ever since William James so defined it. What stirred in the memory of the old soldier was the experience of communal living. Their fellow feeling was largely based on the presence of danger, or the likelihood of it. Butcher observes that in the case of a sudden emergency, a civic catastrophe of some kind, it usually happens that such solidarity is instantly generated; and that in some cases, the experience has brought about a depth of understanding that has led people to change their lives.

In the final paragraph of his short article, Butcher makes a further significant assertion about intentionality in communal life. For the member, this will be a matter of commitment, as stressed elsewhere in this text. His theorem proposes that increasing levels of privacy, powers, resources, entrusted to individuals will not reduce the community's level of communalism *"as long as the equity, or ultimate responsibility remains under collective ownership and control."* That could be a heartening message for the kibbutzim in their present crisis.

Chapter Three

Classical Athens: The Supreme Instance

The scholarship of centuries, millennia even, has focused on Athens. The literature is vast: we may say that for the purposes of this text, we know all we need to know about Athenian democracy, the first in human history, and still unequalled. It exhibits for us almost every aspect and every principle of democratic problems and practice. For this reason, it has been accorded more space in this text than might have been expected.

Classical studies in our time have been sharply reduced, especially in our former grammar schools. This has been an additional reason for registering the Greek achievements, in science especially, which constituted the most brilliant episode in human history. We hope the reader will bear with this: its relation to democracy is central to the argument.

The great French Biblical scholar, Ernest Renan, concluded after twenty years of study that the miracles related in the gospels were open to rational explanation. He asserted that there has been only one miracle in history — that of ancient Greece. Others have reached similar conclusions.

Paul Werner characterised 5th century Athens as the most brilliant moment in the history of humanity: *"this brief period was enough to make Greece the holy land of human civilisation: it was here that human thought was born."* This is hardly an over-statement. It may be that most of the particularities of our high culture had antecedents, yet the development over 2,200 years in so many fields of intellectual activity — philosophy, history, architecture, sculpture, drama, poetry and even natural science — trace their origins to classical Athens. Familiar as this statement is, it continues to amaze us as we contemplate such creativity in a small ancient city. No doubt the materials were to hand, but Greece itself proved to be the super-nova within which the elements of our civilisation were forged.

J. S. Mill affirmed that the beginning of almost every main component of Western civilisation, except for the Judaeo-Christian tradition (and even that in part), is to be found in classical Greece. What critical mass, what chain reaction, underlay this seminal outpouring from a few small towns? This question calls for an answer, and many have been offered, though not all have stressed the evocative power of direct democracy. Professor Jarrett leads into the question with the following:

> *These restless Athenians and other Greeks in lesser degree, impress us with what seems to have been an almost sudden and incredibly great infusion of energy: buildings were built, statues carved, plays written in a quantity — to say nothing of quality — that staggers us. Everyone knows of the marvellous achievements of their sculptors and architects, and we can surmise that their choreographers and composers were also superb, but above all, in the middle of the fifth century B.C. there was a verbal explosion of unprecedented magnitude. Professor Castle claims that the Greek drama was the greatest literary and moral achievement of Hellas — that the Greeks invented the drama. He described how the seven tragedies of Aeschylus (525-456), the seven of Sophocles (496-406), the eighteen of Euripides (480-385) and the eleven comedies of Aristophanes (450-385) which are still available to us, were comparable only to Shakespeare. They were performed before as large a crowd as now attends a cup final at Wembley, seated on stone benches hewn out of the rocky slopes of the Acropolis.*

Let us now identify some of the achievements of Greek science.

The Origins of Science

Science is the unique feature of our civilisation and we owe it to the Greeks. They questioned nature, but they questioned themselves even more. In wondering how they knew anything, they invented and codified logic as a system of rules, representing what we say when speaking of truth.

Thus evolved a standard of rationality, previously unknown, for without logic, there could not have been science.

The Greeks developed the first mathematics by conceptualising number. They did what the practical Chaldeans and Babylonians were unable to do: they were the first to leave the concrete basis and reach a more abstract level.

These pages can offer little more that a gesture of recognition towards the Greek achievement in originating and firmly establishing so many fields of intellectual life. Can we, therefore, allow ourselves to scan a list — incomplete, of course — of their seminal attainments in science and mathematics? Our list will include later Hellenic developments in Alexandria.

Thales (636-546) invented the term "element" and used techniques to calculate distances of ships at sea, heights of mountains, and correctly predicted the solar eclipse of 28th May, 585 B.C. When he visited Egypt, c.600 B.C., he brought back to Miletus geometrical-arithmetical techniques used in land surveying, later developed into deductive abstract geometry.

Alcmaeon of Croton (fl.510) laid the foundations of anatomy, experimental physiology and empirical psychology; dissected and vivisected; discovered the optic nerve; and correctly identified the brain as the central organ of sensation.

Democritus (460-361) was the first to propose that matter consisted of atoms: a speculation that lay dormant.

Polycrates tyrant of Samos, 6th century B.C., fetched Eupalinus, an engineer from Megara, to run a tunnel through the hill of Kastro to make an aqueduct. This was begun from both ends, being 900 yards long, and excavations show that when the two parties met, they were within 2 feet of coincidence. There is, however, no record of their mathematical technique.

Pythagoras (fl.540-510) virtually invented mathematics as a coherent system of relationships between abstracted numbers. At the same time, he invented Western musical theory, linked to mathematics by harmony.

Euclid (fl.328-285): his thirteen books are regarded as the greatest scientific text-books in history — still being used in the early twentieth century. His axiom system of geometry is the first and foremost example of the idea of proof and logical derivation. Historically, his system represents the accumulated labour of generations of Greek mathematicians.

Anaximander (611-546) was first to make a map of the world. Later, and after Archimedes, poles, equator, ecliptic, tropics, meridians and parallels were recognised. Strabo's geographical treatise (c.5 B.C.) explicitly requires understanding of the above concepts.

Anaxagoras (500-428) was the first to commit to writing an explanation of the phases of the moon and had tremendous influence on contemporary thought. But Protagoras was banished, Anaxagoras was gaoled and Socrates put to death for teaching a rational scepticism.

Heraclides (388-310) proposed that Venus and Mercury, never far from the sun on angular measures, revolved around it; and that the daily revolution of the heavenly bodies might be explained, not by their movement, but by a rotation of the earth. (Very upsetting; unacceptable to religious theory of celestial spheres). Heraclides was Athenian.

Eratosthenes (284-192) recorded the altitude of the sun at Assuan and at Alexandria; found a difference of one-fiftieth of the meridian circle; as Assuan was 5,000 stades distance, calculated circumference of the earth at 250,000 stades; which was only 50 miles short of modern measurement.

Archimedes (287-212) wrote texts on the sphere and the cylinder; on conoides and spheroids; on spirals; on the quadrature of the parabola. (Appolonius on Conic Sections brings us into twentieth century mathematics). He calculated the value of Greek pi and also invented the water screw (still used); devised compound pulleys for lifting great weights; invented the principle of the lever; the relation of floating bodies to hydrostatic pressure.

Hipparchus (fl.160-125) revealed the difference between the tropic and the sidereal year; measured the precession of the equinoxes with astonishing accuracy at 1 degree, 23 minutes, 20 seconds. The modern estimate is 10 seconds more. He calculated the positions of 850 fixed stars. He invented trigonometry.

Aristarchus of Samos (fl.c.270) realised that the planets, including Earth, revolved around the sun and that the sun was larger than the earth. At Alexandria, he was the first to propose the heliocentric hypothesis, which was cited by Archimedes and revived, knowingly, by Copernicus. This was too radical for the ancients and only Seleucus, a Babylonian, endorsed it.

Hippocrates of Chios solved the quadrature of the lune — "squaring the circle."

Strato (d.269) fully established experimental technique, claiming primacy over logical argument.

Alexandrian scientists from Euclid to Ptolemy had developed optics (perspective); catoptrics (reflexion, refraction, burning glass); dioptrics (*re* heights, levels, tunnel-boring etc. as our theodolite).

The Alexandrians also perfected a large number of precision instruments. For social usage, a more exact water clock; a water-air pressure pipe organ. For science and research, the astrolabe.

Aristotle (384-322), in establishing the principle of collecting data as necessary preliminary to understanding the physical world, founded the study of biology, which has been called the greatest contribution to science ever made by an individual. But even greater claims can be made for his overall systematisation of knowledge.

On his death, he bequeathed to his followers a vast collection of material on physics, metaphysics, ethics, logic, politics and biology.

He was a pupil of Plato and displayed remarkable competence in the field of idealist disputation while a member of the Academy but, when he moved to the Lyceum, he established a new mode of scholarship which changed the world: he virtually invented systematic research.

He created almost *ab initio* a new science, a logical technique in order *"to determine the limits of validity of the exercise of reason in arriving at a knowledge of reality and in communicating it."* This had not been possible with the Platonic doctrine of ideas.

His biology occupied the last twelve years of his life. **The History of Animals, On the Parts of Animals, On the Generation of Animals,** were *"based partly on second-hand information, partly on original research. He mentions some 500 different kinds of animals; he personally dissected some fifty different types. His newly created logic came into its own."* (Hutten, p.126).

His assertion of the fixity of animal species; his anatomical discoveries; his analysis of moral deliberation and decision-making; his theory of tragedy; his claims for a physiological psychology; these and other writings brought order into human thought and knowledge. More than any other, his work demarcated scholastic specialisms for two millennia. They are still with us.

The Lyceum attracted two thousand students. After Aristotle's death, as Athens continued to decline, the need for an even larger institution of higher learning was recognised, and was established in the burgeoning city of Alexandria under the beneficent patronage of the Ptolemies, whose endowment was maintained over generations of their dynasty. Aristotle's collection of books was transferred to it, and became the nucleus of the famous Library, which eventually attained to as many as 700,000 items, in most of the written languages of the Hellenic world. The teaching centre was the Museum, which had lecture rooms, research rooms, dissection rooms and accommodation for the scholars. There were a hundred salaried professors. This was the world's first great university; why is it not commonly referred to as such? The library and the endowments suffered under Julius Caesar and later under Christian rule, until finally burned on orders from the Moslem fundamentalist Caliph Omar in A.D. 640, when the city was conquered by the Arabs. As a university, it had lasted nine centuries. The production of its original scholars was vast, especially in the first three centuries, after which it fell under the speculative philosophy of the neo-platonists, the gnostics and the early Christian Fathers.

Heophilus proved Alcmaeon's assertion that intelligence was located in the brain, and not, as Aristotle had concluded, in the heart. He also observed the semi-lunar tricuspid and bicuspid valves of the heart; the subdivision of veins and arteries for carrying blood and mapped sensory and motor nerves.

Empedocles demonstrated, by experiment, the existence of the invisible air.

Grammar was a great achievement of Alexandrian science, although the Phoenicians devised the phonetic alphabet. Dionysius Thrax's textbook recognises nouns; verbs; participles; articles; pronouns; prepositions; adverbs and conjunctions and remained in use for thirteen centuries.

The supremacy of the Greek literary and intellectual culture was recognised by the Romans throughout their centuries of dominance and their young men were sent to the academy or Lyceum at Alexandria, and to their credit, they aspired successfully to imitate the Greek cultural production.

The contribution of Greek thought, notably that of the Stoics, was central to the formulation of Christian doctrine. It has been said that every item of Christian teaching can be found in earlier Greek or Jewish literature; that Jesus himself spoke Greek; and that Paul's Greek education is evident in his letters and thought.

The Hippocratic school of physicians on the island of Cos began the scientific practice of medicine.

The Greeks produced the world's first truly naturalistic sculpture and painting. Their colonnaded buildings created the classical orders which were to become a fundamental factor in the architectural styles of subsequent periods: Roman, Renaissance, Baroque and Neoclassical.

In respect of literature and history, one does not speak of the Greek "contribution". In each case, they were the originals, the founding fathers. The names of Aeschylus, Sophocles, Euripides, need no comment. The outrageous comedies of Aristophanes, at last untroubled by censorship, sort well with the works of Dario Fo in our day. Thucydides, Xenophon and Herodotus escaped the legendary accounts of events, and gave us the first histories based on a scholarly accumulation of fact.

Insistently, we ask ourselves why in a loose state the size of Gloucestershire, with a city no larger than Northampton, such genius was generated. Is there some connection with their origination of democracy? The question is worth pursuing.

Acknowledgement: Much of the material for the above section has been drawn from **Greek Science**, Volume I, by Benjamin Farrington (Penguin 1949), and some from **The Origins of Science** by Ernest Hutten (Allen and Unwin).

The Ultra-Democracy

The Athenian constitution carried the principle of political equality beyond what we should regard as its farthest limits. All free citizens, rich or poor, tanner, baker, farmer, plutocrat, or gentleman, had equal right to vote and speak in the Assembly, which was the supreme legislative organ of the city.

This was complete direct democracy in action. Moreover, if poverty made attendance to his political duties too burdensome, the citizen was compensated by a money payment for wages lost. But a more astonishing interpretation of the democratic idea was the custom of appointing state officials by lot — the police, the jurymen, the members of the Council of Five Hundred, the revenue officers, in fact, all officers except the most important of all, the ten commanders of the armed forces. Thus whatever his aptitude or social status, a free-born Athenian would have had experience of every civic office in his city by the age of fifty or sixty. He would have fought in her battles (and provided horse and arms if he could afford it), he would have legislated and judged and taxed, and all this whether he were a cobbler or gentlemen, a moron or a Socrates. Whatever inefficiency might have marred the performance of his duties the Athenian citizen gained first-hand experience of the administrative life of his city. He had felt responsibility, and from early manhood he was learning how to rule and how to be ruled, which is a major part of any man's education. (E.B. Castle, p.34)

Greece is credited with the origination of democracy. Presumably, a collective responsibility in the form of open debate on decisions to be taken had existed among some tribes from pre-historic times. Examples persist in West Africa, and it is said that women are sometimes able to make their voices heard equally with the men in such conclaves. In more developed societies, including very large ones, collective decisions have often been reached, following the death of a ruler, on the election of a new one. This has been a restricted form of participation, usually limited to a small elite and directed towards the maintenance of rule by a single person. The election of the Popes is an instance. Popular opinion may, or may not, be considered, but there is no intention to share power. Democracy is explicitly rejected. The Greeks, on the other hand, endorsed and institutionalised power-sharing. The right of all citizens to take part was affirmed. Rulers and military chiefs were appointed and deposed by popular vote. Anyone could address the assembly on any issue — any citizen, that is. Women, slaves and foreign residents were excluded.

For the present argument, four points call for emphasis:

First, all citizens, or as many as cared to, shared in the decision-making. It involved thousands. It was a direct democracy, not a representative one. This is fundamental: it has been argued that government by a house of representatives suffers from grave deficiencies and is, in fact, undemocratic.

Second, the assembly collectively sought, appointed and supported strong national leaders. There was no wish to limit a leader's power to act by constant consultation. Direct democracy did not impede executive action; rather, it was demanded.

Third, it was successful. Pericles, regarded as among the greatest statesmen in the history of Europe, fully recognised the principle of accountability. He had strong support from the Assembly; and after a most distinguished career, he accepted dismissal by popular vote, following a military reverse.

Fourth, the years of Greek democracy, and Pericles in particular, were the years of Greece's greatest glory. Her architects, sculptors, dramatists, philosophers, mathematicians and proto-scientists formed an intellectual constellation never equalled before or since.

Group theory would associate this tremendous creativity with a system that positively encouraged enquiry, opinion and self-expression. Contemporary accounts describe the Greeks of the classical age as endlessly curious and talkative, in their public places, their dinner parties and their symposia. No doubt a mediterranean climate and poor housing encouraged this. By contrast, Fustel de Coulanges described the peoples of northern Europe as shut in by their need for protection from the weather. Heine was to define silence as a conversation with an Englishman.

In the Greek Assembly there was aristocratic dominance; there were cliques, cabals and conspiracies. It was nevertheless a new thing in history, of immense consequence. It was the first system of open government, partially open at least, in which thousands of citizens could directly participate.

The Democratic Structure

Granted that Solon and Cleisthenes, who drafted the original form, were not fully aware of what they were bringing into existence — how could they have been? — granted that they were more concerned to stave off the threats from aristocratic rivals: this renders even more impressive the functioning of the first sophisticated democracy in history. The possibility of it must have been already latent and awaiting its hour. Peter Green, himself a lecturer in Greek history in Athens, describes its eventual form as follows:

> *"While in the Assembly each man voted on his own, the Council operated through ten rotating tribal contingents, or prytanies, of fifty each. These presided, in turn, as a steering committee, for one-tenth of the year, ie on average, thirty-six days. Lots were drawn daily for a President, or Duty Officer, who, for twenty-four hours, held the city keys and exercised supreme power. Thus, most citizens, during their life-*

time, would participate in the actual business of government ... Though aristocrats, more often than not, continued to occupy posts such as the archonship, they were now accountable to their electors — who took some pleasure in reminding them of the fact. Athenian democracy had, at last, come of age". **A Concise History of Ancient Greece,** Peter Green, (p.94) Thames & Hudson, 1974.

It is hard to discover any self-governing community of equivalent size, and of equivalent administrative sophistication in our century. If any such seemed likely to arise in our own time, it would probably risk extinction by an adjacent great power.

In his account of the Athenian system H.D.F. Kitto writes:

... one was chosen by ballot to be chairman each day. If there was a meeting of the Assembly, he presided: for twenty-four hours he was titular Head of the State. (It happened, Greece being an essentially dramatic country, that Socrates held this position one day towards the end of the war when the Assembly ran amok — as sometimes happened, but not often — and quite illegally demanded to impeach the whole of the Board of Generals for failing to rescue survivors of the successful naval battle of Arginusae. Socrates defied the mob, and refused to put the irregular proposal to the vote). And then we read: "but it was no unusual thing for an Athenian to be a general in one campaign and a private soldier in the next. This was an extreme case of the basic conception of democracy, 'to rule and to be ruled in turn'." pp.126/7.

The random and rotatory element in the holding of office calls for special emphasis. Not only was the President, in office only for a day, chosen by lot; the important Council of five hundred also were chosen by ballot, not elected, and responsibilities were rotated. *"Since this Council was chosen haphazard, and was composed of entirely different people each year, it could develop no corporate feeling. That was the whole idea; nothing must over-shadow the Assembly."*

More surprisingly finance, both imperial and domestic, was tolerably efficient, though this department was run entirely by boards chosen by lot, supervised by the Council, until the latter half of the fourth century.

Surprisingly for us living and working in a stratified society, with all our places of work stratified into manual, clerical, administrative, executive and policy responsibilities; whereas workers in the lower levels are generally capable of the development required for them to function well at the higher levels, when given responsibility.

It is clear that the Athenians of the fifth and fourth centuries intended that the Council should have no chance of developing a corporate sense, which would enable it to take an independent line, the large items and policy issues being reserved for the Assembly of 6,000 or more citizens.

Jarrett's emphasis is in similar terms:

> *Athenian democracy during the fifth century B.C. represents a kind of extreme in this respect that has not before or after been reached elsewhere. Here if anywhere was a government of amateurs, with all ordinary citizens serving as legislators, jurors, executives, bureaucrats and soldiers.*

Sir Moses Finley noted the payment made to citizens for participation in the work of the Assembly, and for other office holders. A drachma a day was paid for the Assembly, four obols for attendance at the theatre. There was also a disablement pension of one obol a day, perhaps not enough to live on, for people of insufficient means. These hard-fought privileges, together with legislation for the regulation of food prices, may well have secured a more equitable distribution of food than one might have expected. Perhaps it goes some way towards explaining Kitto's observation that ten great figures in the music and literature of the nineteenth century averaged a life-span of 54 years. Ten great Greeks from their fifth century B.C. averaged 79. According to Alex Comfort (who has specialised in gerontology), in classical Greece, life expectancy for men and women, the survival rates of children and the stature of men exceeded those of previous and subsequent eras until the nineteenth century; while their dental lesions averaged only 1.0 as against rates of 24 (Rome), 10 (Middle Ages) and 36 for c. 1820.

It was a government of amateurs. There were no permanent posts — distrust of professionals was implicit in the democratic instinct — and some notable examples illustrate this: Sophocles, was placed in command of a naval unit; Thucydides unsuccessfully conducted another; a leather merchant was elected to conduct a campaign and finish it himself, after he had criticised its handling. Socrates was President for a day. There were no public prosecutors in the Courts: private individuals had to bring charges and they brought in slave-constables from Scythia especially to arrest citizens, because it went against the grain for citizens to arrest each other.

In the "demes", or parishes, citizens, on a voluntary basis, performed the tasks of keeping civic registers, collecting war-tax, organising religious rites and supervising the election of State officials. Similarly, the duties of market-wardens, dock-inspectors and collectors of harbour dues were undertaken on a voluntary basis, though probably with adequate remuneration.

Finley again:

> Under the governmental system I have described briefly, Athens managed for nearly two hundred years to be the most prosperous, most powerful, most stable, most peaceful internally, and culturally by far the richest state in all the Greek world. (p.23)

An Imaginative Reconstruction

Each of the 6,000 Athenians knew well that he might have to assume public office quite suddenly, by the operation of the lottery system. Surely this knowledge would concentrate his thinking on political affairs. He would feel a need to know and to understand the working of the governmental machinery. Otherwise he would run the risk of appearing stupid and incompetent; and all the evidence is that the maintenance of public face was of immense importance to the Greeks of that day, and remains so to the Mediterranean peoples in ours.

Let us suppose then that a citizen exercised his right to propose an amendment to some statute in order to correct an inequity about which he felt keenly. Once accepted by the agenda committee (which had rapidly rotating membership) he was free to draft his submission. Imagine, however, whatever the rights of his case, how he might have felt on rising to address the Assembly, and finding himself facing, among the thousands and ready for the debate, most, or all, of the following. We are supposing this to occur during the decade before 400 B.C.

> Socrates, in his mid-sixties
> Plato, in his 20s, might just have qualified
> Sophocles, the grand old man, over 80
> Euripides, in his 70s
> Aristophanes, 45 perhaps
> Thucydides, historian supreme, late 50s
> Xenophon, historian, and authoritarian
> Democritus, 50; discoverer of the atom
> Protagoras, the first sophist, 70
> Antisthenes, stoic, founder of the Cynics, 50
> Ictinus, architect of Parthenon   ) (possibly; their
> Mnesicles, architect of the Propylaea) (dates not certain

There were others whose seminal contributions are enshrined in the literature. Might not that citizen have been forgiven if the slate shook in his hand?

It is clear that the citizens behaved as comrades or members of a team. People were involved with one another as members of a community. It was this predisposition that made possible a successfully functioning democracy, the experience of which in turn reinforced it. It became the central moral value of the culture of Athens over many generations. So it came about that whatever wealth came to the city was expected to be applied for the city's adornment and fame — not for private gratification. The monuments of the Acropolis were the product of public expenditure, openly voted by the citizens to beautify their city, as well as from money donated by the rich.

Pericles described the model city as being a free city, a government of the people, by the people — democracy — with administration in the hands of the many, and not of the few. He spoke of the regular games and festivals and the refinement of their home life: *"Our city is great and open, and all the pleasures of earth flow in upon us and make life pleasant and rich. We do not exclude foreigners; any foreigner may come and go as he will; and the more he learns, the better, for our city is admirable alike in peace and war, and, in a word, is the model city."* He then went on to describe the type of men bred in Athens: all-round men, who were not brutalised to make them strong and who were encouraged to love the beautiful and cultivate their minds, whilst remaining simple in their tastes and retaining their manliness. Men were expected to take an intelligent interest in what went on in Greece, in order to serve their country with sound judgement. He pointed out that the men they counted as brave were those who could calculate clearly the pains and pleasures of life: *"who take the measure of the danger, and then face the risk."*

The idea that the Parthenon and the Erechtheum and the rest were built by a contractor using teams of slaves is false. This great architecture and sculpture were created through thousands of separate contracts: *"one citizen with one slave contracts to bring ten cartloads of marble from Pentelicus; or a citizen employing two Athenians and owning three slaves contracts for the fluting of one column."*

The unfranchised slave, in playing his part in public work, received the same pay as the citizen craftsmen with whom he laboured and, in fact, the great monuments of Athens were fashioned largely by a society of free workers, united by a *"stream of common purpose that partly submerged differences of wealth and birth."*

Professor Jarrett writes:

> *In the middle of the fifth century B.C. there was a verbal explosion of unprecedented magnitude. It is not only that a great quantity of dramatic, philosophical, and historical works were written, but it is as if, at a signal, everybody began talking at once. Men argued, debated, soliloquized, declaimed, contradicted, orated. In trade, in politics, in litigation, in estate management, in war, in courtship, in international relations, he who had the gift of words was victor. Yet, men began to ask, why should we speak of the "gift" or lack of it: are not articulateness, even eloquence, arts (technai), and thus capable of being cultivated, developed, learned — especially if teachers are to be found?*

"No-one has succeeded in accounting for it," says Jarrett; yet he, himself, has juxtaposed the evidence in successive paragraphs. It is only necessary to connect them and to argue that because *"Athenian democracy represented a kind of extreme ... that has not before or after been reached elsewhere"* there followed or accompanied it — of necessity — *"a verbal explosion of unprecedented magnitude ... everybody talking at once ... Men argued, debated, soliloquized, declaimed, contradicted, orated ... in trade, politics, litigation, war, courtship, international relations ..."*

The Great Years

The historical chart on page 34 records the dates, (sometimes approximate), of the Greek writers, creators, historians, artists and philosophers thought worthy of notice in the **Everyman Smaller Classical Dictionary**. The shaded band indicated the democratic phase in Athenian history plus half-a-century, which is intended to recognise that, after the collapse of the democracy, the cultural assumptions of assertion, participation, open speech and argument will have prevailed for a time, even under authoritarian regimes. The names of many writers and philosophers who came from other Hellenic cities or were based more distantly in Sicily or Asia Minor are included because they came from Athens or had lived there for a period in order to learn or, more simply, were heavily influenced by the dominant Athenian culture.

It will be seen that there is a heavy concentration of these originative and seminal figures in the democratic period and its aftermath. By excluding the first twenty years of each life, it becomes possible to reach a sum total of all their productive years within the democratic period, and to make a similar calculation for those whose creative lives fell within a similar period of approximately 135 years after that. This calculation gives approximately 1,430 productive years within the democratic phase, and 830 for the following period. The strongest evidence comes from a chronological tabulation of the formative years of those selected for the dictionary. If one regards the years 10 to 25 as most significant for the development of a mental set towards intellectual dialogue and creativity, noting how many had their formative years in the 120 years or so before the democratic phase, how many during that phase or its aftermath , and how many during the post-democratic equivalent time-span, one finds:

Pre-democracy	9
Democratic and after-math	36
Post-democratic	9

The Democratic Era
Working before:

700	Homer	
	Hesiod	
600	Archilochus	
	Thales	
500	Pythagoras	
	Sappho	
	Alcaeus	
	Anacreon	
	Anaximines	
	Heraclitus	
	Simonides	
	Cleisthenes inaugurated democracy 507	
400	Aeschylus	
	Sophocles	**Dramatists**
	Euripides	
	Aristophanes	
	Herodotos	**Historians**
	Thucidydes	
	Andocides	
	Isocrates	**Philosophers**
	Socrates	
	Plato	
	Xenocrates	**THE DEMOCRATIC ERA**
	Xenophanes	
	Prodicus	
	Empedocles	
	Praxiteles	
	Phidias	**Architects and**
	Ictinus	**Artists**
	Mnesicles	
	Myron	
	Polycletus	
	Callicrates	
350	Aristotle	
	Diogenes	
	Demosthenes	
	Lysias	**CULTURAL PERSISTENCE**
	Xenophon	
	Gorgias	
	Protagoraxs	
	Antisthenes	
	Apelles	
	Callimachos, and probably	
	Lysippus	
	Scopas	
	Aristippus	
200	Theophrastus; Menander; Pyrrho; Theocritus; Epicurus	
0	Polybius; Posidonius; Agasias	
100 AD	Epictetus; Arrian; Plutarch; Zeno	
300 AD	Lucian; Pausanias; Plotinus; Porphyry	

Assessments

Feminist claims for the rights of women are historically recent, despite the occasional voice that speaks to us from past centuries. Eighteenth century France was more than two thousand years distant from classical Athens on the historical time scale. Some distinguished women were accepted in Athens; Aspasia was not unique. But in general, the Athenian view of women was one they shared with every other advanced culture of the time and in the succeeding millennia. It is unrealistic to expect the Greeks to have taken alone the vast imaginative leap into our changing perceptions. In any case, where in the twentieth century has sex equality been achieved? There are enough instances of discrimination in our time to offer targets for feminists. They have no call to single out the ancient Greeks.

Assessments of Athenian democracy continue to appear, and no doubt will do so as long as history is written. A recent one is by Mogens Herman Hansen, published in 1989 by the Royal Danish Academy of Science and Letters, under the title **"Was Athens a Democracy?"**. Dr Hansen convincingly demonstrates his main thesis that the Athenian democratia resembled our modern forms in being a set of institutions and ideals; and that their concepts of liberty and equality in civic rights were close to ours; also that democratia as ideology was remarkably close to the political ideals of western liberal democracy. He is not especially concerned with the opposition between direct and representative democracy, but he clearly recognises it: *"there can be no denying that direct democracy is more 'democratic' than representative democracy."* He attacks the modern champions of democracy who do not discuss this issue, brushing the direct form aside as fit only for small urban centres. But, *"already, although teledemocracy remains only an idea, opinions are sharply divided, and its implementation would undoubtedly bring back the ancient dispute about the merits of popular rule"* and he calls our attention to the fact that as late as 1848 the Swiss federal constitution, which embodied both, saw democracy and representation as direct opposites. This is close to the position taken in this book.

Some would argue that the cultural/historical gulf between classical Greece and our own life-world is so vast as to preclude the possibility of our understanding the perceptions and motivations of the citizens of Athens; that the concepts on which they constructed their thought-systems, and the meanings of the words they used, cannot possibly be brought to life again; and that the more we attempt it, the greater the risk we run of murder-by-dissection; of self-deception, in that the further we attempt to penetrate, the more likely we are to construct a picture composed of our own pre-conceptions. Such warnings are salutary; we need to work with these possibilities in mind. The reality is, however, that the histories of Thucydides, the great tragedies and the great philosophies, sculpture and architecture of the classical age make an impact upon us. We resonate to them strongly, and we cannot help doing so. We know that we share with them a great deal that we accept, too easily perhaps, as a common humanity. Too easily, because when we attempt to assimilate what has come down to us from the great civilisations contemporary with classical Athens in India, China, Egypt or Mesopotamia, while we discover great works that compel our admiration, we do not have the sense of sharing the warmth and fullness of human experience as with the Greeks. This, perhaps for two reasons: first, the Athenian civilisation was the embryo of our own; second, others reflected their hierarchical systems based on absolute power, whereas the Greeks reveal to us endless disputation and individual difference, leading even to tragic consequence.

Further, they analysed their experience, as others did not. All of that is something we understand.

With the Poetics of Aristotle and the Harmonics of Aristoxenus the basis had been laid for an intelligent and conscious criticism of the nature and function of art. The human spirit had made immense gains in its consciousness of itself.

Stone's Question

I.F. Stone was a radical journalist of some fame in the United States over a period of fifty years. He did not easily accommodate himself to the job opportunities available to him, and he eventually founded **I.F. Stone's Weekly**, a news-sheet which ran for nearly twenty years, up to the time of Watergate, and was much valued by other journalists because of its unusual perspective and items of information.

On retirement at the age of seventy, he taught himself classical Greek and embarked on a study of Athenian democracy. His focal interest was in freedom of speech. No doubt this had always been a matter of personal importance for him, because he had necessarily sailed very close to the wind in exposing to view so much that powerful figures would have wished to keep under wraps. He spent most of his last ten years writing **The Trial of Socrates**. He was seventy when he began it — the same age as Socrates at his trial — and eighty when it was published; as was Sophocles when writing some of the first very great tragedies in western literature.

I.F. Stone wished to understand how it could have happened that Athens, famous in its own day as in ours for receptivity to all ideas and their often exotic exponents, could possibly have sentenced to death in open assembly their most famous disputant. In brief, his argument, massively buttressed by evidence, is that Socrates was not fundamentally sympathetic to democratic rule; that his negative dialectics were destructive of the faith that the young might have in its values; that Athens had twice within a few years of the trial experienced the horrors of a brutal aristocratic dictatorship (in 411 and 404 B.C.), achieved with the help of Sparta, the enemy that eventually destroyed Athens and ended the democracy. The aristocratic coup was led by Critias, one of Socrates' most brilliant and favoured pupils.

As for free speech, I.F. Stone's penultimate paragraph reads:

> *So from the sixth century B.C. to the sixth century A.D., philosophy enjoyed freedom in Athens. That was twelve hundred years, or about twice as long as the period of free thought from the Renaissance to our own day.*

Stone clearly demonstrates the association between the continuing creativity of Athens and its generally prevailing freedom of expression; with its sustained reputation as a university city through the centuries of the Roman empire, and with the duration of the Academy (Plato) and the Lyceum (Aristotle); and with its overwhelming creative brilliance during the two centuries of participatory democracy. That was the historic moment when, as a minute embryo, the processes of intellectual growth and differentiation began which have now attained to such scale and such power as to overwhelm us in our time, unless we achieve some collective coherence in the face of our extraordinary contemporary situation. Stone regards freedom of speech as the basic socio-political value. What then is the relation between freedom of speech, freedom of thought and democracy? Psychologists and anthropologists have examined the relation between speech, language and thought. For instance, can deaf-mutes, who are likely to remain illiterate, be capable of conceptual thinking? Given that the answer is positive, we may still assert that socially and culturally, language and thought are reciprocally inter-dependent. Cultural development has increasingly depended upon the written word, and in recent centuries on printing. The freedoms of thought, speech and publication are seen to be inseparable. Long-term suppression of certain proscribed ideological or literary content has affected collective thinking over generations. The question that remains concerns the relations between freedom of speech, freedom of publication and democracy. The ideal type will simply assert that democracy is directly and wholly dependent on freedom of speech and publication. Development theory, both marxian and liberal, has assumed that where such freedom can be brought about, a collective demand or participation in decision-making political processes will be generated. Historians, who are necessary disinclined to accede to general assumptions, may be content to state that in the histories of all nations all freedoms have been partial, that the outcomes can never be understood in unitary causality and that all is relative. To this we may assent, and we would lay stress upon the conclusion that all democracies so far have been very limited, even the best of them. In our time we may be tempted to think that the more democracy is claimed and proclaimed in the West, the more fraudulent it appears.

Sparta: the negative instance

Is further evidence required? One might look for contrast at the culture of the Spartans. Theirs was an independent city state comparable with Athens. Conservative Athenians looked towards Sparta with admiration and envy. It was an authoritarian state par excellence. The hardship and fierce discipline imposed on the young was emulated, though not equalled in Athens. Their military prowess was especially regarded, and rightly feared; they finally defeated the Athenians in the Peloponesian war, thus extinguishing their independent and democratic lifestyle, and exposed them to occupation by the Macedonian Philip II. The Spartans had a senate, and an assembly of all citizens. But they were not allowed to debate. Decisions were arrived at by shouting — the loudest shout carried the day. The Athenians were amused.

The Oxford English Dictionary defines *"laconic"* as brief, sententious, concise, severe. The derivation is from Laconia, which was the Spartan territory. The Athenians referred disparagingly to the Spartans' brief, laconic style of speech. Perhaps they assumed that Spartans had little of interest to say, and in this way they were right, if we are to judge by the paucity of their literature. It may be argued that if a culture discourages the expression of what is original, what is not traditional, even in conversation, then nothing new can be created. If a new thing is not to be discussed, it will cease to be thought. If there is to be no new thinking, there will be no new thing. This was the condition that the Athenians correctly identified with Laconia.

The history of our own century tells us clearly enough that rigid authoritarian regimes suppress creative intellectuals and artists. The history of the Jews and the fate of their most distinguished scientists and writers demonstrates the point. In point of fact, if one were to seek for a social order, with a relatively small population, having a record of quite exceptional cultural contribution to the twentieth century, the Jewish people would surely emerge as pre-eminent. This is not to say that, even with such great names as Freud and Einstein, whose work permanently changed our understanding of ourselves and of the physical world, the Jewish contribution could compare with that of Athens, from which the intellectual life of the western world so largely arose.

The present argument is that, in the thrusting of responsibility onto free citizens, debate and original thinking were necessarily entailed: and that the precipitate and wholesale experience of direct democracy gave the great stimulus to Athenian intellectual activity and thereby to western civilisation.

This account of the Athenian polis leaves our contemporary representative mass democracy, so sedulously sold to us as a freedom worth fighting for, even at the risk of nuclear holocaust, exposed as a charade. It is better understood as a system that marginalises its own population, frustrates democracy in the name of democracy, clears the field of action for a small self-interested elite and disseminates only partial information. Only direct participation on the Greek co-operative model could offer some hope of a transformation of our social life.

Decline

The Athenian democracy slowly degenerated into a battleground for competing factions. Brilliant successes against the vast Persian fleets and armies at Marathon, Plataea and Salamis preserved the independence of Athens in 479 but left it full of hubris, and too ready for war against the Peloponnesian League a generation later (431). The unsettled interia had left the citizens disgusted with the ruthless manipulation of the democratic system. As always with groups living through a phase of confusion and fragmentation, there was a longing for a (good) strong authoritarian leader, who could determine and impose policy. And, again, there were strong leaders to take command after Pericles.

Successive military defeats eventually exposed the Athenians to the dominion of Philip II of Macedon. The old elite and their great authoritarian intellectuals, Aristotle and Plato, who shared a dislike for democracy and favoured a return to aristocratic rule, were now able to observe government by a strong man, not exactly one whom they would have chosen.

> *Intellect, now, had entered the service of absolutism, with which it had always had a social, class-based sympathy. Aristotle may refer only in passing to Philip or Alexander in the politics, but their great shadows lie across every page ... the strong men, whose sharply dictatorial swords slashed through the more-than-Gordian knot of fourth century Greek politics, the shattered coda of what, for all its faults, had been the most exciting and progressive political movement yet known to mankind.*
> Peter Green, *op.cit.*

In spite of a few outstanding instances of moderation and true nobility, it is on the whole a melancholy record of degeneration under the stress of war and opportunist leadership: and Thucydides' tragic history should be read for what he intended it to be, not merely a record of what a particular people did in these particular circumstances, but an analysis of human behaviour in politics and war. (H.D.F. Kitto, p.148)

Salient Points

Athens has been the only state, or city state, to run itself as a direct democracy and to do so over so many generations. For this reason, it offers an excellent base on which to construct the general case for self-government. It will therefore, be appropriate in concluding this chapter to identify those primary components of their system which can be seen to have relevance for possibilities in our time; relevance which may prove to be trans-historical, even a permanent validity; but for the present purpose we select the following.

1. It was the outcome of a long struggle by the citizens against the slave-based wealth of the aristocratic land-owning classes who would have preferred an oligarchy, or even a tyranny, in the Greek sense of one-man rule. Further, the democracy had to be vigilantly defended against possible coups by aristocratic juntas, which were in fact temporarily, and murderously, successful in 411 and in 404.

2. For geographical-historical reasons, Athens had become the polyglot talking shop of the ancient world. The citizens enjoyed, literally enjoyed, and valued, complete freedom of speech.

3. The Assembly governed by a complex super-structure of administration, law and appointment to office; but the principle was firmly maintained over nearly two centuries that even the highest elected officers were

instantly accountable to the Assembly, which frequently exercised its right to remove them from office. Power remained with the citizen body.

4. The Assembly was familiar with the election method, which was in regular use. However, a high proportion of officials throughout the system were chosen by lot, even the President who held office for one day only. The system was devised to ensure the widest possible distribution of responsibility.

5. By successive experience in the courts, in financial administration, in regulating commerce, in arranging for religious festivals, the great dramas, or the Olympic games, most citizens had acquired an extensive knowledge of government by middle life, and military service will have been a requirement from the age of eighteen. All such experience was explicitly viewed as the appropriate training for participation in public affairs. The implications for education are profound.

6. All historians of Greece have noted that the decades of supreme creative brilliance were coincident with the best years of the Athenian democracy. Our discussion of the principles of self-government leads us to propose that the relationship is causal rather than coincidental.

Chapter Four

Quakers

300 years Without a Leader

The most impressive example of an anti-authoritarian leaderless system, surviving for more than 300 years, is that of the Quakers, the Religious Society of Friends. Their self-managing conduct of affairs, in meetings large and small, has changed little since the early eighteenth century. Their practice reveals an unexpected sophistication and theoretical interest.

The Society remains small, at around 18,000 members — a figure which has varied little during the last century. Its influence has penetrated and ramified to an extent out of all proportion to its numerical base. There are, however, 12,000 attenders, whose numbers are increasing. Yet there has not arisen from amongst them any instrument of propagation of their group method in its general significance.

Under the powerful influence of their charismatic founder, George Fox, they sought for truth within their individual experience, in revulsion against the doctrinal wrangles of the conflicting protestant churches following the Reformation. Such a revulsion was widely felt in the early seventeenth century. It was not merely that the varieties of doctrine were felt to have little relation to the lives and circumstances of the less educated laity. It was also that the churches and their clergy were seen as living on the backs of productive citizens, notably through the tithe system. Furthermore, corruption in the Anglican Church had often resulted in the appointment of uninterested or uneducated, sometimes illiterate, priests.

Adult educators will recognise the significance of something else. Following Caxton, printed books were becoming widely available. Among these, the Bible had first place (and still does in the annual lists of best-selling books). Early English translations were superseded by the splendid authorised version of 1611. The wish to read the Bible for oneself, rather than relying on the parish priest's account of it, was a strong motive for literacy. Reading led towards every variety of Biblical interpretation and practice. There were

Ranters and Antinomians, who rejected all moral prescriptions. There were Levellers and Diggers, who found in the Bible inspiration for radical social programmes. Theorists and pamphleteers of astonishing insight took advantage of a relatively free press. Many of Winstanley's pages, for instance, read like an anticipation of Karl Marx. When Christopher Hill, then Professor of History at Oxford, wrote his famous book on this historical period he did not invent his title: **The World Turned Upside Down.** It seems to have been a phrase widely in circulation, especially among the fearful establishment. Kruschev was by no means the first to discover that, as people receive more education, they become more democratic.

Self-determining religious groups proliferated. Some, notably the Baptists and the Congregationalists, insisted that each of their churches should appoint and pay their own chosen ministers to expound the Gospel, to preach on Sundays, conduct modified rituals, to lead and care for their own.

All of this was rejected by Quakers, especially by George Fox, who imposed the requirement that they should choose to have no leaders; at least, no permanent paid leaders, appointed to have authority over them. In itself, that was an important historical break; but the principle of individual and collective responsibility was even more so — its significance can only be fully appreciated in our times.

Practitioners and theorists in group dynamics observe that, if there is no leader, as when from the start the person appointed to take the group will not assume the leader role, a search for structure manifests itself. Bids for the leadership from among the members are made, but set aside. An absent, symbolic or dead leader may, however, be acceptable: his demands can be interpreted so as to accord with the general consensus of the group. The dead leader is felt to be alive, and present in spirit — the normal religious position, which the Quakers share. Furthermore, his first followers will have recorded his words, which become a sacred text, a statement of ultimate truth. The text substitutes for the presence of the leader. The task of the group is then to consult the text on all salient issues, and to interpret it. This is the position adopted by all fundamentalist sects. Many will have the additional blessing of an appointed, or self-appointed interpreter of the text. The felt need for such guidance is clearly very powerful, as is evidenced by the born-again Christians in the United States or the popular support for religious leaders in Moslem countries.

Knowing that the Bible appears to *"say"* one thing in one place and a different thing in another, Fox asked his friends: *"But what canst thou say?"* This was a moment in cultural history. For people who had lived under the authority of church and state in all things, now in a new world where rival sects presented their own claims to authority, to be told to reach their own judgement on the basis of their own inner experience, must have come as a great liberation and, at the same time, a total challenge.

When groups accept that there is no formally designated leader having authority over them, a general sense of heightened responsibility comes to be shared by all individual members. This is as evident in groups which have come together to learn about themselves as in producer co-operatives. It happened with Quakers. Without priests, without creeds, or dogma, without altars, images, sacred buildings, or Sundays seen as different from any other day, each person was thrown back on his or her inner (but transcendent) resources, and supported by others committed to the same practice.

There were several significant outcomes. Perhaps the first was a recognition of individual differences, a mutual respect and acceptance that, as others are different, their inner experience and ways of thought will also differ. Such mutual regard and toleration is the basic building block for all democratic practice.

The interchange of views is a powerful corrective to eccentricity and idiosyncrasy. Without argument, without debate, which are expressly excluded in agreed Quaker practice, the regular re-discovery of the differing perceptions of other concerned and well-informed people on immediate issues can result in profound self-questioning. It was enough to make a person quake, when s/he has been feeling most sure. George Fox said something to this effect to the judge (though invoking the name of God) at his early trial, which gave rise to the name.

Practices of self-management in the local group, co-ordination at regional level and at the yearly annual meeting, open to all members, had to be hammered out. This, again, was largely achieved by George Fox, who travelled widely in Britain and Ireland for the purpose. In the three centuries since then, the structure and practices of Friends have not greatly changed.

Collective Responsibility

A connection between direct democracy and Athenian creativity was proposed in the previous section. A more direct connection can be claimed in Quaker history. From their early necessary concerns with care for the distressed and persecuted, and for prison reform arising from their experiences in every generation, their contributions to social welfare and policy, extending currently to ethical investments, have greatly exceeded what might have been anticipated from their small numbers. Professor Alastair Heron has stated the position as follows:

> *Our book membership of 18,000 implies not more than 12,000 Friends who can be described as active members in most ordinary senses of that word ... across the area of the Yearly Meeting we have an average of one continuing attender for each two active Friends ... Against this background, it cannot be gainsaid that the quantity and variety of our creaturely activity in dealing with our corporate and personal affairs, and in the doing and stimulating of good works is out of all proportion both to our active numbers and to our spiritual resources.* (Friends' Quarterly, April 1989).

The vast proliferation of local initiatives and local investments in response to need by other bodies precludes the possibility of comparative quantification. A perusal of the annual reports of Quaker Social Responsibility and Education, touching on homelessness, unemployment, the elderly, poverty, AIDS, penal affairs, community relations, mental health, apart from the well-established international action for peace and for third-world aid and development, fully substantiates Alastair Heron's assessment.

The acceptance of a degree of responsibility by all Friends led the Society to pioneer valuable initiatives in several fields. Each of the following has its own history; most have received extensive documentation. In each case, it would be useful, but sometimes difficult, to identify the role of Quakers in association with others. It appears that Quakers were among the prime initiators in all cases. In other instances, the lead passed into different hands and Quakers have lost all connection and influence. This has happened in the later histories of some of the best-known banks, and some of the famous chocolate firms.

Commercial Ethics

First in historical significance was the Quaker adoption of complete probity in the conduct of business. The spoken word had to be honoured. The long-standing 'Advice' to Friends was to ask themselves: *"Are you honest and truthful in word and deed? Do you maintain strict integrity in your business transactions? Are you personally scrupulous and responsible in the use of money entrusted to you?"* A price was to be named and there was to be no haggling, no bargaining. The transaction was to be seen as a straightforward exchange, not as a contest in which each tried to get the advantage. Such an ethical practice had been advocated often enough on Sundays and disregarded on Mondays. Quakers refused to regard Sundays as special; all days were to be lived in truth and love. They were the first who established this conduct of affairs in the open community.

The consequences were almost immediate. Fox observed that people tramping from town to town in search of work, no doubt finding their footwear in need of repair after a pounding along the rough roads, would ask: *"Is there a Quaker shoe-maker in this town?"* It was found that a child could be sent to a Quaker sweetshop or grocer with a half-penny, and would receive full measure. This, of course was very good for business. Quakers tended to prosper, because of their good reputations, straight dealing, regular lives and frugal habits. They had also learned, of necessity, to be prudent, in a world which was, for them, very dangerous.

So it was made manifest that honesty is the best policy, a sentiment that Samuel Smiles later endorsed. But the Friends did not behave honestly for policy reasons. They would have repudiated such calculation. They were honest because they felt that the Lord had required it of them. They expected, rather, that their directness of speech would bring trouble and suffering upon them, which it certainly did. They were prepared for poverty; and when many of them achieved prosperity they were not entirely sure what to think about it. George Fox recognised this dilemma in the first generation of Quaker maturity. The dilemma was never resolved.

Social Initiatives

Penal Reform

From their earliest days, Quakers had been subject to legal oppression, mostly because of their repudiation of the established Church. This was severe, even under the merry monarch, Charles II, when thousands were thrown into the appalling prisons, where hundreds of Quakers died. Friends reacted by establishing their Meeting for Sufferings, to do what could be done to help their fellow victims. It has now met monthly for more than 300 years and is never short of business. It has become the central executive board of the Society: it functions with 200 members.

This early experience led Friends into their concern for prison conditions. John Howard, a pastor, had earlier publicised the hideous conditions in gaols and had secured legislation for sanitary and other improvements, seldom enforced. Elizabeth Fry, a Quaker, became the pioneering reformer, especially in relation to women prisoners, and an international figure. Friends have continued to be familiar with prison life, because their pacifist stance, currently with forms of anti-nuclear protest, frequently brings upon them short prison sentences. It cannot be said that the movements for prison reform have been successful during the last half-century. Conditions are deteriorating, perhaps world-wide.

Care of Mental Patients

A most notable Quaker innovation was the opening of the Retreat at York for the reception and humane treatment of the insane. This was a most necessary reform running directly counter to the prevailing practices of chaining and whipping and exposing these unfortunates to public ridicule. The Retreat still runs and has a high reputation. William Tuke was the prime mover. He shared his concern with York Friends, and the Retreat was founded as the result of their collective decision.

Non-Violence

Then there is the Quaker peace testimony. When one considers the bloody history of Europe and its colonial wars, the conscription of vast populations to engage in them, the death, disease and destitution which they brought, then revulsion must be universal. The Quaker position on peace no longer appears far out, or unrealistic. On the contrary, it appears increasingly to be a realistic option and ultimately, perhaps, necessary.

Concern for Workers

The provision of humane conditions for workers was pioneered by the Quaker chocolate firms: Frys, Cadburys and Rowntrees. The Bournville estate was built for Cadbury employees. Of course, it proved to be too small for an expanding labour force; and there were the usual problems related to retirement, unemployment, change of employment.

In the hard times of the 1930s, Dame Elizabeth Cadbury was said to receive a surplus worker into her office, shake his hand, thank him for his contribution to the company, present him with a well-bound Bible, and a redundancy notice. No-one has seen this as an adequate response to the contradictions of capitalism: the Achilles heel of Quakerdom, perhaps. The humane attitude is seen to be insufficient, and no principled critique of liberal capitalism has been agreed by Friends. An endorsement of the participative co-operative forms of enterprise might be possible for them, because of its political ambiguity.

Ethical Investment

A recent innovation has been the inauguration by the Friends Provident Insurance Company of Britain's first ethical Unit Trust, which refuses investment in companies with substantial interests in South Africa, in the manufacture of armaments, the production and distribution of alcohol or tobacco. This has been successful, even in terms of yield. There had been several precursors in the United States. Friends Provident is not a Quaker enterprise although some Friends were involved in its foundation.

The Quaker Enterprise

The Darbys of Coalbrookdale developed the use of coke and applied steam pumps to recycle water. Their initiative attracted scientists and engineers from many countries. Ironbridge is their monument. Another Quaker family, the Lloyds, dominated smelting, the processing, distribution and sale of iron goods in the Birmingham area. Such was their commercial success, they needed to establish a bank to provide credit for their customers: the development of Lloyd's bank is history. Quakers were prominent as bankers or treasurers in the production of rails and in the founding of railway companies.

Quakers were responsible for the world's first railway. David Windsor invites us to speculate on what the industrial founding fathers might have thought of the later developments, naming such Quaker families as Barclays, Huntley and Palmers, Crossfields, Wedgwoods, Wilkinson, Jacobs, Rowntrees, Cadburys, Frys and Terrys. It must be said, however, that although they provided their workers with somewhat improved conditions, they were not pioneers of participative democracy within the firm.

The social initiatives listed above are, perhaps, enough to demonstrate that the Society has been more creative, relative to their numbers, than comparable bodies. It seems that they have committed themselves more purposefully, and more consistently, to respond to changing needs and distresses. Their record is so eminent that it invites a speculative explanation.

Friends would wish to believe that anything they have achieved and done springs from their practice of opening themselves to the inner movements of the spirit, informed directly by God, without mediation of any kind. It is possible to suggest, as briefly indicated above, an explanation in less exalted group dynamic terms. This would rest on the observation that where there is no leader, group members, of necessity, take responsibility on themselves. The argument of this text is that this gives rise to a constant flow of task-centred thought and action; and this may be seen in the industrial, educational, political and therapeutic fields.

The Observation of a Jesuit

In the early 1980s, Michael J. Sheeran, S.J., was permitted to undertake a three year Ph.D. research programme of investigation into the Quaker mode of self-management. He was concerned to observe the processes of voteless decision-making, to talk with many of the members and to discover the divide between those who believe in guidance and those who do not. The following extracts have been chosen because they illustrate well what has been said above. The clarity and meticulous honesty of his account will speak for itself. He prefaces his text with a paragraph from Rufus M. Jones' book of 1932, significantly named **Mysticism and Democracy,** focusing on the decision process among Friends.

The central idea was the complete elimination of majorities and minorities; it became the Quaker custom to reach all decisions in unity. The clerk of the meeting performed the function of reporting the corporate sense, ie the judgement of the assembled group, and of recording it. If there were differences of view, as there were likely to be in such a body, the consideration of the question at issue would proceed, with long periods of solemn hush and meditation, until slowly the lines of thought drew together towards a point of unity. Then the clerk would frame a minute of conclusion, expressing the sense of the meeting.

Later, Sheeran quotes from Thomas S. Brown a passage equally indicative of the quality of a Quaker meeting and of their decision-making processes:

It is also of great importance that those Friends who feel they cannot speak acceptably and who are diffident about the significance of their share in the Meeting be encouraged to say what they can, remembering that the concerns they feel they present so haltingly may in fact point to issues needing the Meeting's consideration.

Another sign of this same power is the reply we often received to questions about how a clerk ought to proceed if there is clearly a united meeting with the exception of one or two people who refused to stand aside for reasons the clerk has judged insignificant. One clerk spoke for many: 'It happens fairly often. If the time is available, hold it over. If an immediate decision is needed, then I, as clerk, would ask, "May we record your objection and proceed?" If the person is in his right mind, he'll say yes. If he is just plain unreasonable, then you make up your mind according to the factors in that individual case'.

It became clear, however, that the clerk is the instrument of the general will, the sense of the meeting.

The Friends' sense of their collective reliance on the leading of God, Christ, the Spirit, the Inner Light, is problematic. Sheeran writes:

> *... the puzzling difference in perceptions on this occasion seemed compounded as the researcher attempted to discuss with Friends their individual understandings of the religious significance of Quaker decisions.*

He soon found himself enmeshed in a world where everybody seemed to use the same vocabulary but with different meanings.

Quaker understanding of how unity is reached and the significance of their decisions can be confusing. One says the group has reached Truth, meaning Truth is the guiding light of Jesus Christ. Another finds in Truth the best aspirations of man but dismisses references to Christ as *"baggage from another age"* when people didn't know better. If four Quakers agree that Christ is the Truth which guides Friends, then for one this means that Christ is the historic Jesus, for another a name for the Creator, for the third an impersonal force, and for the fourth a euphemism for the relief one feels when one has tried hard to be honest in making a choice.

No matter how contradictory the language sounds at first, it all points to a mutually-shared event: Friends experience something special and invoke some privileged explanation to indicate why their type of decision is different from ordinary ones. They find an authenticating dimension outside the mechanics of the process.

One Friend, a professional political scientist himself, commented: *"I doubt that a common goal plus acceptance of the rules is enough ... There is need of a bona fide religious myth, a mysticism, to which people really feel subordinate."* p.73.

Meetings for business are, in principle, not different from meetings for worship. The period of silence which begins and ends the business meeting expresses this, as do silences called for during a meeting, when difficult or conflictual issues present problems. It will be argued that this practice may have group dynamic significance, whether it is experienced as an act, of worship or not. It is strikingly different from the more familiar voting procedure.

It may sometimes be equally shallow or perfunctory. Sheeran, having in mind a large annual meeting, when hundreds may be present, observes:

> On the formalistic end of the spectrum, the initial silence seems about as significant as the chaplain's invocation at the Democratic National Convention. At the opposite pole, however, one thinks of occasional meetings — or parts of meetings — when the comments of individual speakers were followed by long spontaneous silences for prayer and the observer felt himself drawn into the group's profoundly worshipful seeking.

Such a worshipful situation is occasionally accompanied by surprising shifts of position, either by individuals or by the entire group. An example from the American Friends Service Committee may be helpful. In an interview, one former AFSC staff member recalled:

> In 1948, there were 750,000 refugees on the Gaza Strip; the new state of Israel had just been established. The UN asked AFSC to take responsibility for feeding, housing, etc. At the meeting of the AFSC Board of Directors, all speakers said the work needed doing, but all agreed it was just too big for the Service Committee. They counselled that we should say no, with regrets. Then the chairman called for a period of silence, prayer, meditation. Ten or fifteen minutes went by in which no one spoke. The chairman opened the discussion once again. The view around the table was completely changed: "Of course, we have to do it." There was complete unity.

Some Quakers have said that the large London Yearly Meeting does not work very well. Nor do other annual meetings of a similar size, in the experience of this writer. They may appear to work smoothly through an agenda, with satisfaction all round, as might be the case with a successful company's shareholders' meeting. To those of us accustomed to participatory processes, they are felt to be profoundly unsatisfactory.

Church Government the Friends call their book of guidance, which approximates to a set of rules, or regular practices. But in historical fact, Quakerism had its origins in opposition to all established churches: the term "church" is misleading, as they apply it to themselves. One might have the impression that their book of government was a set of non-rules for the non-government of an anti-church. It is the method, based on shared personal attitudes, that is of the essence.

Quaker practice recognises not only the ethical dimension of great public issues but also of personal interaction in the decision-making group. By contrast, the absence of ethical reference in the general literature of chairmanship, committee work, even in group work is conspicuous. It demonstrates how far the conduct of affairs has separated itself from a concern for human values.

And how much has been lost thereby:

> *Particularly remarkable was the treatment of the Indians by Penn and the Quakers. In striking contrast to the general treatment of Indians by white settlers, the Quakers insisted on voluntary purchase of Indian land. They also dealt with the Indians as human beings, deserving of respect and dignity. As a consequence, peace with the Indians was maintained for well over half a century; no drop of Quaker blood was shed by the Indians. Voltaire wrote rapturously of the Quaker achievement: for the Indians, he declared, 'it was truly a new sight to see a sovereign William Penn to whom everyone said 'thou' and to whom one spoke with one's hat on one's head: a government without priests, a people without arms, citizens as the magistrates, and neighbours without jealousy'.* (In **Libertarian Analysis**, Vol.1, No.1, p.28, New York, 1970).

In 1656, when the group practice of the Friends was beginning to crystallise, the elders at Balby issued an epistle with the following postscript. It has been frequently quoted, and still is. It expresses well the relation between prescription and intuition basic to their culture:

> *Dearly beloved Friends, these things we do not lay upon you as a rule or form to walk by, but that all, with the measure of light that is pure and holy, may be guided; and so in the light walking and abiding, these things may be fulfilled in the Spirit, not from the letter, for the letter killeth but the Spirit giveth life.*

For present purposes, the following points may be recognised as salient:

The Society of Friends effectively managed its affairs for three centuries without formal leaders.

Their decision-making process rejects majority rule, rejects compromise, and even the seeking of consensus. Their methods have some similarity to what, in group dynamics is called *"working through"*.

They have been the first to recognise the value of silences in the making of difficult decisions.

Their groups have a distinctive quality deriving from a recognition that the *"leadings of the spirit"* may lead Friends in opposed directions with equal validity. Discussion is superseded by personal testimony.

The effect of leaving an unmediated responsibility with the individual or the meeting appears to have generated a plethora of valuable social initiatives.

Comparison with the leaderless T-group method suggests that a cardinal issue in group work and in democratic process lies in the management of conflict.

Quaker method is normative; that is its essence. The Friends are not so much concerned with the efficiency of their method as with how people ought to behave towards each other. The method appears to be efficient in respect of difficult and long-term issues; less so with everyday operational items.

Sheeran describes the Quaker mode of decision-making, in which polarization is avoided by withdrawing one's opposition but not one's disagreement, as virtually *"an art form of graciousness"* (p.67). No more generous and exact assessment could ever be offered by a Jesuit priest or by any observer.

A recent article, entitled **Quakers: a Leaderless Group**, by B.P. Dandelion, may be found in the Friends' Quarterly, April, 1993, Pub. Friends' House, London, N.W.1.

Chapter Five

Self-Government in Industry and Trade

Most of us prefer to have the essential facts on any issue, and to work out our own conclusions. For this reason, the following chapter presents brief accounts of successful, sometimes astonishingly successful, partnerships, commonwealths; co-operatives; as they may choose to be called. All are enterprises which have firmly established themselves within economies dominated by rapacious competitors. Authorial perspectives and interpretations will be evident at many points — not too intrusively, one hopes. The final sections offer interpretative comments, and point up some fundamental questions.

The National Freight Corporation: a Spectacular Success

The arrival of the N.F.C. on the co-operative scene was like a sunburst: this, for three main reasons. First was the scale of the operation, rising from 10,200 to around 30,000 members. Second was its commercial success following conversion. Third was its historic superiority over state ownership, on the one hand, and free-ranging capitalism on the other. It sets up some challenging questions for all political parties and philosophies at present on offer. The number of workers involved is estimated to be three times as many as the total of all other co-operatives in the U.K.

The conservative government of 1979 wished to privatise the loss-making N.F.C. but its prospects were so dismal that financial advisers recommended postponement of proposals for flotation. In 1980, senior executives, led by Peter Thompson, planned a worker buy-out, asking for a minimum of £200 from each — more from those of senior status. Persuasive publicity was organised and 10,200 employees (including the families of some, and also some pensioners), accepted, contributing an average of £600. Existing share capital was bought from the state for £53,500,000. Large sums had to be raised by loans and by support from a bank syndicate, to meet the purchase price. This generous financial assistance was, no doubt, the key factor which made the buy-out possible.

By the end of 1988, when a carefully controlled share issue was floated on the Stock Exchange, there were 27,200 employee shareholdings and a further 18,000 in the names of families or pensioners. At the time of the buy-out in February, 1982, an ordinary share was valued at 2.5p. By November 1988, the value had risen to 185p.

Many hundreds of employees found that their holdings are worth between a quarter and a half million pounds. This, surely, is something to concentrate the mind wonderfully, as did the earlier prospect of redundancy. Diversification has led to purchase or consolidation in four Divisions: transport, to include B.R.S., Lynx Express etc; distribution to include N.F.C. contracting, National Carriers, Fashion Flow (for Marks & Spencer); home services — Pickfords house removals, Allied Van etc.; and travel — Pickfords again, part of Lunn/Poly etc. There is also a property group which brings good returns.

All of these divisions are in profit, yielding, in 1987/88, £3.6 million from travel to £32.1 million from transport. Overall profits totalled £90 million on a turnover of £1,255 million. (A loss of £35 million had been recorded in 1976). This is a spectacular co-operative success at the level of very big business. Despite the economic down-turn, profits had increased towards £94 million by 1993. The fear has been that, following the further price rise after flotation, some of the workers would be tempted to realise their gains by selling to outsiders, which was not possible before the Stock Exchange listing. The Stock Exchange authorities allowed the worker/shareholders double voting rights — against the resistance of City firms. The N.F.C. directors feared that, if too many of the workers sold their holdings, the City firms, or one of them, would build up a block of shares, use their influence at shareholders meetings and, by progressive increase, eventually take over the Consortium in the name of private enterprise and to their own great profit. The weighting of voting rights in favour of the worker/shareholders should be enough to block this development for a long time. It must serve to reinforce employees, in the sense that the huge enterprise really is theirs.

It also marks a break-through in Stock Exchange practice. It opens the gate for other successful co-operatives which may wish to follow the same path. But, beyond this, there is the matter of simple equity. In every generation since the industrial revolution, the cruel injustice resulting from the rights of remote shareholders or finance companies to close a factory, even a large business, without consulting the workers, whose entire lives and families may be dependent on it, has received bitter comment. The recent decision sets a new precedent that could be followed, even in private firms which think of themselves as following enlightened personnel policies.

N.F.C. *"declares that its philosophy is to extend its activities, to acquire other companies, mainly overseas, to seek sustained growth in profits* (1993)".

There is the matter of payment of directors. Sir Peter, at 60, moving into a consultancy role, received £99,000 for a three-day week, over twelve months, reducing to £66,000 for two days in the third year. His terminal full salary appears to have been £127,000. He owns around 1.6 million shares, worth more than four million pounds. *The Guardian's* financial commentator regarded this as a *"relatively modest"* return for having built a £1,255 million business. And, of course, as recently as the buy-out of 1981/22, he had to raise a £40,000 mortgage on his own house to provide his share of the original risk capital. But it stands in contrast to Don Jose's declaring for a 3-1 ratio between the highest and lowest rates of pay, though the ratio in Mondragon now extends to 7-1, as does Commonwealth (see chapter 6).

Very high salary levels are beyond the imagination of most of us, and appear uncalled for. There are, however, mitigating considerations. First, to receive a high salary is honest because it is open and heavily taxed (though much less than was once the case). Second, there is the problem of a reward structure. The skilled worker, the supervisor, the assistant manager, the departmental manager, all expect to receive payment that reflects their greater responsibilities. The structure continues upwards through the groupings and divisions to top management, director, assistant chief and chief executive. Each differential must be significant: a person promoted to a post of greater real responsibility, often felt to be demanding and anxiety-creating at first, will react with disappointment, perhaps de-motivation, if the differential is felt to be insignificant. By this logic, in a very large undertaking, with extended hierarchical structures, the chief executive must have a very high income, however he may judge it in terms of equity.

Sir Peter is disappointed that so few companies have followed the N.F.C. example. *"We have thousands of management buy-outs but, apart from a few bus companies, hardly any owned by employees."*

The Directors attribute a considerable part of N.F.C.'s financial success to the commitment of the employee/shareholders. The N.F.C. philosophy of employee share ownership is based on two fundamental principles:

> *employees should be encouraged and assisted to acquire shares in the*

Company because they are thus able to identify themselves more closely with N.F.C., to the benefit of morale, motivation and profitability; — employee shareholders ... should have more influence over major decisions than shareholders whose investment alone is at stake. (N.F.C. Annual Review, 1981 and 1982).

Interest-free loans of £500 are, in fact, available to new employees for buying shares. Interviewed by *The Observer* (29.1.89), Sir Peter Thompson spoke more directly about his own philosophy. He praised his school experience, especially at Bradford Grammar School, where *"we were taught by this great left-winger called Gus Shepherd"* who believed that nationalisation would solve everyone's problems. He himself would have liked to believe that, and he sought employment in British Steel and, later, in charge of B.R.S. (British Road Services, a part of National Freight, established by Barbara Castle, with 63,000 employees). From this followed the possible privatisation, to which he responded by initiating the co-operative proposal, as described. *The Observer* interviewer sees him as still inspired by a socialist idealism; yet he, clearly, became disenchanted with nationalisation, and other sources have quoted him as seeing in the flotation *"the chance to spread the gospel. Popular capitalism is really working."*

Unlike so many who reach top management, his feeling for his workers has positively increased. This must have provided the driving motive which led him to persuade his colleagues and to take the plunge into a new world of co-operation.

The 1992 Annual Review announces *"our ambition to become one of the world's foremost international businesses."* Their extension into Germany, Belgium, France and especially the U.S.A. gives substance to this intention, notably by the performance of their logistics division — warehousing and distribution. Their operations extend to 20 countries, involving 20% of their 32,000 employees.

During the year of recession, they made 1,650 employees redundant. Smaller co-operatives, eg Scott Bader, will not in fact do this, even at the cost of shared reductions of pay. This gives us the indication that N.F.C. is not in essence a co-operative. It is an E.S.O.P — one which has spectacularly demonstrated the token effect. Employees have strongly identified with the firm, from which they have greatly benefitted, but do not control. They own around 20% of the equity. This has been contrasted with the total ownership and control, by way of full meetings, of the Scott Bader company: but N.F.C. is one hundred times as large as Scott Bader, which limits itself to around 350 employee members. Some have confidently predicted that N.F.C. workers will sell their share holdings, and the whole undertaking will revert to the conventional status of international corporations.

The John Lewis Partnership

As John Lewis or Waitrose, this large enterprise is very well-known in all the areas of Britain in which its eighty supermarkets and more than twenty department stores are located. It is a closed corporation in that all employed in it become Partners on joining. It is totally owned by the 32,000 Partners. Unlike the National Freight Corporation, with which it is in some ways comparable, it has no share capital traded on the Stock Exchange. The welfare of the Partners is at a high level. The salary-plus-bonus system puts them well above payments offered by their commercial rivals for similar work. Security is high; there are generous holidays, leisure facilities (four cruising yachts), large subsidies on the purchase of tickets for symphony concerts and the theatre.

Until recently, the chairman, himself a Lewis and of the original family, appears to have had almost total power. He directly appoints top management, who remain accountable to him. It would seem, therefore, that in the John Lewis partnership we have an example of old-style paternalism, comparable with the best of the nineteenth century Quakers and others. The recently appointed Stuart Hampson, a civil servant by origin, may bring a different style.

One is impressed by the immense flow of information, available to all Partners. Much refers to the Council, and the work of Councillors. A large structure is revealed, which channels an upward flow of opinion, question and sometimes challenge. This is a feed-back system on a large scale. Questions, and full replies from the appropriate members of senior management, are published in *The Gazette*, which is the monthly house journal.

Of course one may ask, what is the effect of this flow and counter-flow, if management reserves for itself the right to decide? The answer must be, that here we have a large corporate system in which the Partners elect their representatives and clearly enjoy freedom of information, opinion and expression. They behave as if they believe that what they have to say does have some effect on the thinking and action of senior management. It seems unlikely that they are deceived in this. It would appear that freedom of information and freedom of speech are the essentials. As said elsewhere in this text, there is a sense in which a co- operative may be said to exist if its members feel that it does. It is the feeling that energises their collective behaviour.

In the history of the John Lewis Partnership, and the Company that preceded it, one notes a principle of personnel selection that may have some bearing on the above, and certainly on overall management. During the first half of the century, even later with some concerns, one could observe odd and irrelevant criteria in common use. It was thought important, for instance, that the candidate should have attended a particular type of school; or advantageous if he had a sporting record; or certain family connections. Even in the 1950s a large steel company, poised for nationalisation, chose their executives largely on appearance. The chairman was satisfied that he could distinguish the right sort of candidate by the way he (never she) walked across the room on entering. Furthermore, he liked big men, who looked as if they could carry a steel girder on their shoulder. Once appointed, all were required to wear a navy blue suit, a dark red tie and a glimpse of handkerchief in the breast pocket. After which, one is relieved to read that the John Lewis looked for good honours graduates, which may well have been one determinant of their commercial success against fierce competition.

In 1979, Spedan Lewis sold his controlling interest in his company to a trust representing present and future workers. The enterprise became entirely employee-owned. It has a turn-over of around £1,500 million and profits approaching £100,000,000. Of profits after tax, more than half are distributed to employees as a bonus, amounting to 20% of their salary. Employees also benefit from five weeks annual holiday and index-linked pensions.

The study from which the following facts are taken, by Keith Bradley and Saul Estrin (PRL, 1986), compares the performance of the Partnership with that of its main competitors and co-equals in scale. These are Sainsbury, Marks & Spencer, Great Universal and Tesco. As these great names are synonymous in the public mind with driving efficiency and relentless competitiveness, the findings are of some interest. They are presented in tabular form, and with great sophistication. Taking the fifteen year period 1970-85, they report:

> *sales in the Partnership grew at 7% p.a.; faster than those of its main competitors;*
>
> *its productivity growth rate has been higher than theirs;*
>
> *wages paid before bonus were among the highest in the group; profits*

show a long-run trend in excess of 4%. This is higher than that of most of its competitors.

For our present purposes, we must ask how far ownership entails participation. This is a question we also address to the National Freight Corporation. It appears that both of these very large concerns take great care with the dissemination of information to their worker- partners; and that there is a committee structure, with an elected membership, who maintain some oversight of affairs. We shall argue that much more than this would be possible, and in all probability, even more profitable, for these enterprises. The accountability of senior management to their staff could be the key issue.

An abstract from a long standing declaration of principle reads:

Sharing Power.

In the conduct of the Partnership's affairs there shall be as much sharing of power as may be consistent with properly efficient team-work. The Partnership's recruitment shall be aimed at securing individual and collective capacity for successful democracy.

Sovereign authority is intended to be in the Partnership's public opinion, which shall be enabled to influence the conduct of affairs in various ways: by means of formal arrangements for sharing knowledge; by personal contact, formal and informal; by mass-voting or referenda covering either the whole of the Partnership or particular branches or selections; and by the use of representative bodies, composed of elected or appointed members.

1844

Every U.K. citizen has some experience of the Co-op., and some knowledge of its principles and methods. The image of the Co-op, long ago became established, a part of the national collective unconscious, we might say. And as Freud insisted, the unconscious has no sense of time: what is lodged there is fixed — unless dragged painfully into consciousness. The Co-op., in fact, constantly changes, but cannot change its image. (Does not the great Woolworth corporate have a similar problem?) Will Leo, Living, Home World, Late Shop succeed in creating new images? Competitors may realise that the old giant is not sleeping. Familiarity would preclude even an outline of the present structure and complexity of Co-operative Movement as at present. Co-operative Retail Service is the largest Society, accounting for 18% of all members and 21% of all co-operative sales in Britain, have a membership of 1.44 million, and a turnover of £1,285 million (1991 figures). Members' share capital was £62 million — not enough, one might think, to stir such a body of members to action, though it is claimed C.R.S. is largely controlled by them.

If the above percentages may be taken as a base for extrapolation, we have to think of seven millions of our population as enrolled members within the whole movement. These figures are not static. From 1987 to 1991, turnover increased from £1,052 million to £1,370 million; trading surplus from £24,300 million to £44,864 million.

C.R.S., and the Co-operative Retail Societies throughout Britain are not workers' co-operatives. Workers do not own or control these enterprises. From 1844 onwards, Societies were formed by and belonged to their members; that is, their customers. It was the intention of the founders to promote producers' co-operatives. This they did in 1854 with the Rochdale Co-operative Manufacturing Society, a textile mill. This was so successful it was able to raise money for expansion by issuing shares. These were rapidly bought by outsiders, and the venture was lost to the Co-operative movement — an early example of the perils of success.

Spain

Mondragon is the world's most famous co-operative entity. It is a linked system of enterprises, including industrial units, banks, schools and colleges. The policy has been not to enlarge the central unit when opportunity occurs, but rather, to hive off autonomous, but related, new ones. The start was as recent as 1956, when a handful of disenchanted graduates from the local technical college, founded by a priest, Don Jose, consulted him about the possibility of setting up a co-operative, based on a small metal-working enterprise they had started. This was successful, partly owing to the support of the community of Mondragon, in Basque country. Perhaps they have special reasons to appreciate the virtues of solidarity.

By the 1980s there were more than 80 linked co-operatives, focusing on household cookers, refrigerators, etc, but also producing a wide range of other goods. There are now more than 12,000 members. The bank, having branches throughout Basque territory, has deposits of $500 million. On joining the system the new member is asked to contribute $4,000; the bank will lend it to him or her at a moderate rate of interest. Presumably there is a high level of participation, as the AGM is held in the football stadium. Annual turnover approaches £1 billion.

The co-operative took over the technical college which now provides some university-level courses, and has 1500 students. These are regarded as an essential resource for the varied enterprises.

Don Jose was insistent on collective responsibility. His influence determined the bottom/top earning ratio as 1/4.5; but this has since been increased. He died in 1976, but his inspiration is still significant for the practice of the many units.

Senor Jesus Larrenaga, one of the founding fathers of Fagor, Mondragon's oldest and largest enterprise has said that if he had to advise on the setting up of a similar unit today, he would not recommend a co-operative unit. Sol Enoch, who was in conversation with him, believes that the success of Mondragon has entailed the process of "goal displacement". *"The quest for efficiency and competitiveness clearly overrides the original goal of a co-operative ideology, such as equalitarian wage structure."* E.g. the wages ratio has slipped from the original 1:3, to 1:5, or even 1:7. Profits are re-invested in the enterprise, rather than in social capital, such as housing. *(Bulletin of the International Communal Studies Association* No. 8, 1990).

The best available assessment of the Mondragon achievement is that by Hans Weiner and Robert Oakshott for the Anglo-German Foundation in 1987. Significant points relevant for the present argument include the following:

There must be rules to ensure that a co-operative does not fall into the hands of external finance capitalists, by controlling share sales, or limiting them to members of the extended "family". In Mondragon the workers own all the capital, more than half in the form of shares, the remainder belonging to the collective; but about half of the working capital is in the form of bank loans — which puts the bank in a strong position. The bank is, of course, itself a part of the Mondragon complex. At the start, in 1960, there were four co-operatives with 395 members. By 1985 there were 111 with over 19,000 members, with sales reaching 141,000 million pesetas.

Technology has become more specialised and the markets more international. It has been necessary to call in expert advice, which raises questions for the overall wage structure. A total welfare, housing, health and pension system is in operation for all members and their families.

Absenteeism runs at about half the level of that in comparable firms. There have been a few necessary redundancies, but far below the prevailing norm. Some of the co-operatives failed, but it was usually possible to deploy the workers elsewhere.

The origins of Mondragon were educational. The initiative arose out of the League of Education and Culture, founded in 1948, in the technical college. The college, itself a component of the Mondragon complex, now trains graduate level managers. A statement in 1993 of Dr Antonio Concelo, who directs the Mondragon supermarket chain, reports a doubling of sales in four years, and an expectation of taking on an extra 7,000 workers during the next four.

Japan — a Women's Story

Japan is too much presented as macho, authoritarian, right-wing and corrupt. How agreeable then, to read in *Resurgence No.128*, an account (originally in *The Guardian's Society Tomorrow*) of the formation of the Seikatsu Club in 1965, by a Tokyo housewife.

We are told:

> The traditional co-operative movement in Japan has a similar history to that in the UK and elsewhere: the collapse of producer co-operatives as industrialisation gathered momentum and the consolidation of agricultural and consumer co-operatives into more or less conventional marketing, distribution or retail businesses. Thus little remained in Japan of the original vision of the Rochdale Pioneers ...

A Tokyo housewife decided to found the club in order to cut down on costs by co-operative buying. In the beginning, her intentions were no more radical than that *"but as awareness rose in Japan, as in other countries, of the ecological and social costs of industrialism, so the Club's concerns aligned themselves with this awareness"*. With a share capital of 13 billion yen and retail sale of 71 billion yen, membership of the club in 1993 totals 218,000 households, serving 500,000 people and *"as it has grown the movement has become more committed to goals of social transformation as well as of consumer benefit"*. The Club was explicitly based on the example of the Rochdale Pioneers.

In 1974, they began ordering soap powder from producers to replace the synthetic detergents that were polluting Japan's waterways. Food safety also became an important issue, resulting in close links between the Seikatsu Club and Japan's growing organic agriculture movement. When Club members found that it was impossible to buy additive-free milk, for example, they set up their own minimum processing plant linked to some organic dairy farms and distributed the real milk produced direct to members throughout the Tokyo metropolitan area and its suburbs.

The growth of the Seikatsu Club during the seventies and eighties has been *"phenomenal"*. Members *"are organised in 'hans' of no more that seven to ten people, autonomous local groups which make purchasing decisions and initiate broader Club policy on the basis of members' wishes."* 100-150 hans form a branch and branches *"are organised at the prefectural level, which is the major unit of Japanese local government."* There are 35 branches in the prefecture of Kanagwa, south of Tokyo, which have a purpose-built six-storey headquarters, designed by a member. In this building, there are *"traditional Japanese rooms at the top, a gymnasium, a theatre/cinema ... meeting rooms, offices, both an alternative and conventional health centre, a second-hand shop, wholefood restaurant, pre-school nursery and several small businesses in the food/health/education sectors."*

In Japan, *"housewifery is a recognised profession"*, with wives having *"total control of their husbands' salaries, which will normally be paid directly into the wife's bank account or handed over to her unopened by the husband if it is a cash-packet. The husband may then get an allowance, but only after the wife has planned the household's saving, investment and consumption strategy."* Therefore, the great majority of Seikatsu Club members are women and the organising impetus comes from those who are full-time housewives. The part-time staff of more than 200 has a more equal proportion of men.

Now that the number of women in full-time employment is increasing, the *"volunteerism of the Seikatsu Club is gradually being replaced by paid employees, organised into workers' collectives, again mainly women."* Thus, the success of the Club is mainly due to the *"formidable business skills of Japanese women."*

The approach of the Seikatsu Club has several interesting features:

First, they seek to integrate the roles of producer, consumer and investor. It is important for their consumers to have a direct and personal relationship with their producers. They seek to understand the production process and the producers' problems, are concerned with workers' conditions, management style and ecological impact. In the food sector they visit organic farmers and often help to take in the harvest under their direction. Prices are not set by the market, but directly negotiated between producer and consumer, giving the former security of income, and the latter an opportunity to influence what is produced and how. If they cannot find a producer who will conform to their standards, the Club will consider starting its own enterprise, using funds raised through membership subscriptions and interest-bearing Consumer Co-operative Bonds.

When the Club became aware of the political dimension of their work, they tried, unsuccessfully, to influence local politicians and then *"took to the hustings themselves with the slogan 'Political Reform from the Kitchen'."* In 1979, their first member gained a seat in local government and *"Now there are 31 elected members in three prefectures, all women, called Agents of the Seikatsu Club and organised in a network that is linked to, but distinct from, the Club itself. The women inspire confidence that they can root their high ideals in the everyday world of ordinary people."*

E.S.O.P.s.

The Treasury publishes a booklet entitled *Sharing in Success*, claiming that one in five of the work-force now belongs in some scheme of profit sharing, which has tax advantages. It enables employees to buy the company's shares at reduced prices, and of course to share in its profitability. Employers like it because it reduces their wages bill. But this means that if the firm has an unprofitable year, the workers' wages drop below the going rate for the job. Furthermore, pension rights will be insecure, or only as secure as the firm itself.

E.S.O.P.s (Employee Share Ownership Plans) are popular in the United States where ten million workers are enrolled. In some cases, workers have come to own a majority of shares, attend share-holders' meetings, and vociferously press their demands. This is said to work wonders for their motivation on the shop-floor. In Britain, however, the proportion of worker-owned shares has declined since the war. Most ownership is institution-based whereas E.S.O.P.s are likely to succeed with small or medium-sized firms.

Perhaps for structural reasons, E.S.O.P.s, and outright worker-ownerships thrive in bus and transport undertakings. The largest has been the West Midlands P.T.A., which has inaugurated a complex system of progressive buy-outs, with in-built safeguards against hostile take-overs. Others have been Yorkshire Riders, Busways and Grampian — where, in each case, management reserved for itself 51% of total shares. The National Freight Corporation, the largest and most successful undertaking, operates in a comparable field. The National Bus Company announced their intention to sell off the unprofitable network between Southampton and Portsmouth. With help from union leaders and consultants, the workers planned their bid, asked for £750 from each of their 212 employees, and got it. The new managing director is a former bus conductor. The change in attitudes and fortunes has been *"electrifying"*, according to report, particularly in reliability and customer relations. Where a private firm has fallen into difficulties and is threatened with closure, the opportunity may present itself for a buy-out because the firm's marketable assets may attract a bid from outside, with a view to a quick return on the sale of site and buildings. Against this a defensive buy-out may be planned by the existing management, whose contracts and reputation enable them to secure temporary loans to add to what they can raise among themselves. Such a bid may in turn fail for one reason or another, in which case, there may be a possibility of a bid from the workers. A modest amount from each of them may well outrange the resources available to the managers. The chance of retaining one's job can be a strong incentive to a worker to raise perhaps £500 from some source. Two hundred workers might raise £100,000 by this method, in a firm where six managers could find no more than £50,000. A workers' co-operative may thus supplant a projected managers' co-operative.

In scanning the evidence for collective self-government, the question insistently arises: is this a genuine example of collective decision-making, or is it a mere token of the sharing of power?

There is, however, one effect which we need to bear in mind. This is that the token, the symbol of power-sharing, is often sufficient to generate some of the good consequences claimed for self-government. It may be that this token effect is sufficient even to preserve one form of representative democracy, whose spurious claims have been outlined above. If one finds that the proportion of genuine co-operation in a large enterprise is small, its effects may still be large, especially where there is honesty and openness in the meetings of executives and operatives. The above accounts, brief as they are, may be enough to raise questions of that kind. The social history of the United States is rich with accounts of self-governing committees and enterprises. The literature is too vast for summary, and none is attempted here. The co-operative tradition is very much alive at the present time, partly as a reaction to ever- increasing unemployment. The best-known recent example has been that of Wierton Steel, which, faced with the threat of shut-down, was bought by its 8,500 employees. It was successfully turned around, and was prospering within three years, despite the notorious over-production of steel world-wide.

Great Men?

Those with a simple faith in the works of great men will have their ready-made response to the above accounts of industrial co-operatives. They will short-circuit the discussion by insisting that Don Jose, Spedan Lewis and Peter Thompson were remarkable men, combining great practical acumen with vision and charisma. That was no doubt the case, but is not of itself a sufficient explanation for all that followed. It was not any vision that inspired them: it was a correct vision. It is the historical function of great men — let us rather say: men with a great vision — to demonstrate the validity of their truth. These were more than prophets: they were practitioners. They showed the practicability of a genuine alternative.

Chapter Six

Co-operatives

There have been successful co-operatives in every generation which left no record of themselves. Some, of which we have records, are unjustly neglected. The medical doctor, William King, aroused hostility from the rich, and from his patients in Brighton, by establishing what is claimed as Britain's first co-operative in 1827. It was successful, and was able to pay its workers 14 shillings per week, where 10 shillings was the norm. Within three years, this example had given rise to 300 co-operatives, before King yielded to pressure and returned to his practice. His achievement influenced the Rochdale weavers in 1844.

This chapter gives some brief data on smaller co-operatives in different continents, some of which have formed networks, unions or political parties. There is some discussion of the question of scale, which presents immediate structural problems for co-operatives, but is less significant for commitment and morale than might be expected.

Co-operatives and Bureaucracies in the U.S.S.R.: A Historical Episode of the Gorbachev Era

Problems in Communism was a bi-monthly publication of the U.S. Information Agency. The following paragraphs on New Co-operatives in the U.S.S.R. are taken from an account by Anthony Jones and William Moskoff in the November 1989 number. The general picture is one of headlong growth amid a maze of difficulties. It seemed likely that bureaucratic exigencies would extinguish their greatest potential, leaving them in a marginal role relative to the main economy.

The C.P.S.U. had cautiously facilitated co-operative development. By 1987, 8,000 had been formed, employing 88,000 workers, their production estimated at 134 million roubles. The Party hoped for more. A marked tendency was towards conversion of unsuccessful state enterprises. An unwelcome challenge to those responsible for the unsuccessful units could be foreseen at this early stage.

In 1988, a law on co-operation was adopted, permitting them to own private productive property. It instructed government authorities not to prohibit or interfere with the co-operatives. No limit was set to their size, and they were even permitted to employ part-time workers — a significant ideological departure. The resulting growth was phenomenal. From 8,000 to 14,000 in 1988, and then:

Jan. 1989	77,500	employing	1,392,000
April 1989	99,300	employing	1,950,000
July 1989	133,000	employing	2,900,000

Another 100,000 were in preparation, and registered. The rise in output was even more dramatic.

1987	350	million roubles	
1988	6	billion roubles	
1989	12.9	billion roubles	(June figure)

This amounted to 2-3% of all goods and services, from 1.5% of the total 130 million workforce.

Whereas co-operative workers were approximately 1% of employed people in Estonia (significantly), in the Moslem republics (Turkmenistan Azerbaijan, Tajikistan) the proportion was less than one-fifth of this figure. Our section on Cultural Variable in Chapter Ten, stresses the compatibility of some cultures with co-operation, rather than others. Probably, the Moslem culture will prove to be resistant to this, as to other contemporary movements. The status of women will be significant where matters are resolved in open debate. But the possibility of that debate will be a cultural factor. Co-operatives will be excluded from cultures which teach that all social and economic questions are to be settled by reference to ancient texts.

The success of the co-operatives in the U.S.S.R. engendered hostility among many workers leading impoverished lives. They saw that the incomes of co-operative workers were greater than their own, often by as much as 50%, with bonuses in addition. Further, co-operative restaurant meals and retail goods cost up to three times as much as those on offer in the state system, and were not notably better in quality. But they were available, which means everything in conditions of chronic shortage. The consumer saw the co-operatives as contriving to rob the state of what should have been made available to all at a low price. They were seen as the very model of rapacious capitalist development that the worker was taught to abhor from his school days onwards. The top management of Soviet co-operatives often played into this perception by paying themselves very high incomes, or taking capital gains of hundreds of thousands of roubles. Furthermore, it was known that co-operatives have often been penetrated by criminal networks. A functioning co-operative can be a cover for dealing in stolen spare parts, illegal imports or drugs.

In the day-to-day running of their affairs, however, the co-operatives were most troubled by the indifference, or hostility, of the officers of state. Co-operatives are dependent on the state banking system for start-up loans. They complained that these were always too small, and too short-dated for purposes of capital investment. Then they had to find premises. These would often be left-overs from state enterprises which had failed, or been closed down. A planner, of course, might declare premises no longer available at any time. If the co-operative were successful in business, that fact would not endear it to the state functionaries who had failed. Then there was the problem of obtaining materials. As virtually everything is state property, the decision to sell scrap metal, fuel, electronic equipment or whatever to the co-operative would lie with one or other official. He might change, or his sympathies might change. His judgement might be arbitrary, or he might be looking for a percentage of some kind.

It was clear that the powers of the bureaucracy were quite sufficient for them to eliminate any, or all, of the co-operatives within their domain. The functionaries might well consider that it would be in their interest to do so, rather than to allow an alternative to their own administration to grow so rapidly in size and power. Why did they not do so? Perhaps because many of them were genuinely trying to implement the law of 1988, in spirit as in letter.

Rural Co-operatives

It has always been evident that groups of workers are capable of co-operating in their own interests and of collectively managing small undertakings. The early examples were mostly in agriculture. It became clear to small farmers that their dependency on commercial interests could be mitigated, even obviated, by combining to form marketing and purchasing systems for supply of seed and fertiliser, equipment, transportation and, significantly, credit. The scale of the combined operations gave them a commercial influence which, as individual agents, they were seriously lacking. Co-operatives have proved themselves to be suited to the needs of the small family farmer in all continents, although to a varying degree. A substantial proportion of agricultural produce has been marketed by co-operatives in Germany, Scandinavia, France, Spain and Italy, as we may sometimes observe by reading wine labels. That local co-operatives should themselves collaborate or combine for larger purposes was politically significant. It made possible the creation of co-operative farmers' parties with their own orientation, equally opposed to the urban industrial/financial hegemony and to its proletarian-socialist alternative.

Farmers' co-operatives have also established themselves in Latin America, in Africa and in Asia, though nowhere in those continents have they succeeded in defending peasant economies, with their associated life styles, against the depredations of highly capitalised agro-business. It begins to look as if rural life will everywhere be swept away during the next generation, its people displaced rather than re-settled, drifting by necessity to the terrible peripheral sprawl around the great cities.

It is not surprising that rural co-operatives, even large ones, could not stand up to the mass purchasing, mass retailing methods of the big systems. An example: the women of a rural co-operative in Trinidad, aided by a technical teacher, were found to be producing attractive and original artificial flowers. The visiting buyer from the United States said: *"Yes, we could sell those in our department store. How long would it take you to produce a thousand dozen?"* In each instance, the efforts of the rural co-operative will simply be by-passed, and later extinguished, by the large urban systems.

In other instances in India, Latin America and Africa, co-operatives for poor or landless peasants, which might have achieved something, have been broken up by the strong-arm agents of local land-owners. A successful co-operative would have threatened their nearly absolute power and ultimately, their wealth. It would have been an intention of the co-operative to achieve a reduction of the near-feudal power of local elites, necessarily so. This may be taken as a local paradigm of what can happen on a national scale if a co-operative movement appears to offer a successful alternative.

An International Enquiry

In 1975 the U.N. Research Institute for Social Development published their investigation into the performance of several hundred rural co-operatives in India, Sri Lanka, Africa and Latin America. Their findings were dismal overall, but not hopeless. We may take the timing of their enquiry to mark the growing disenchantment with the top-down model, the assumption that collective development could be brought into being by specialist planners from government, international agencies or charities. A decade later, the same institute was to publish quite different reports describing a small number of successful programmes largely based on local initiatives. The need for such a concept as conflictive participation was also argued.

The 1975 report exposes the factors at work determining the failure of so many projects to achieve a general advancement in the condition of the impoverished majority. The great majority of the co-operatives at that time, many of which had been established decades before, had been taken over by the more prosperous and powerful members of the local community, and operated to their benefit. The poorest landless peasants were excluded from influence, even from membership. Leadership was often corrupt. This pattern was found to be the case especially where the social structure was stratified, exhibiting large inequalities of wealth and income. The credits made available by the funding agency or by local savings were commonly subverted to meet the capital needs of the richer members: in any case, they were better able to manage the accounts.

It seemed to be universal that the co-operative structure reflected or reproduced that of the local social system. Where the community of origin was more egalitarian, the co-operative had more chance of successfully meeting its aims. Even there, as in all three continents where male dominance persists, the co-operatives were so dominated; the situation of the women declined, as many of their traditional functions to do with the production of food were taken over by the co-operatives.

The general conclusions were as follows, therefore:

The impact of the community structure upon the co-operative appears to be stronger than the impact of the co-operative upon the community structure.

In general, the effectiveness and viability of the co-operative as an institution appears to depend to an important extent upon the relative homogeneity of its membership and the absence of sharp class and caste barriers in the community from which the membership is drawn. (p.103)

If such co-operatives cannot be expected in most cases to benefit the masses of poor rural inhabitants, then this should be made quite clear, and measures more appropriate for these groups should be considered in rural development programmes. In their present circumstances many rural communities would appear to provide highly unsuitable environments for the introduction of co-operatives as agents of overall development, and instead of attempting to implant co-operatives in such environments government efforts would be more usefully directed towards bringing about desirable social, economic and structural changes by means directly aimed at overcoming obstacles to rural progress. To that, we would all wish to say: So be it. But to ask a government to bring about such changes when it may have been elected, or have seized power, exactly to prevent them, as most have, is a weak conclusion.

The key problem is often the ownership of land, or access to it. Many countries, especially in Latin America (eg Brazil) have legislated for land re-distribution, with minimal effect. Indeed, they have been unable, or unwilling, to prevent the illegal seizure of the peasants' land by violent means. What is the point of setting up a co-operative in such a situation?

In the communities studied, the U.N.R.I.S.D. report stated that although there were increasingly large numbers of landless labourers, particularly in Asian countries, the co-operatives did little to tackle the problem. Examples were given showing that, at the time of the study (July, 1976), 88% of the members of the four co-operatives studied in Ceylon were landowners, although 40-50% of the villagers were landless; and 98% of the co-operative members in East Pakistan were landowners, as were 86% of those in West Pakistan.

The report has nothing to say about the general failure of population programmes. It is obvious that where populations have doubled in a generation, the mal-distribution of land and its use by large land-owners for export crops, will be catastrophic. U.N.R.I.S.D. will not allow a totally negative conclusion:

Land distribution was not so unequal in two co-operatives in Ceylon and economic controls were not influenced by caste. In these, interpersonal trust among members was of a higher degree and corrupt practices, such as those indulged in in other Ceylonese and Asian co-operatives, were not engaged in by the leadership.

No doubt, conclusions of this kind, and many arising from studies of development initiatives not defined as co-operatives moved thinking towards grass-roots participation and decision-making in the community. What is involved here is a process of empowerment. This entails some loss of power on the part of those who are presently powerful and, therefore, will be resisted. Further, the local elite will usually have quite sufficient power to prevent it.

It is usual to find that any proposal for the re-distribution of land is fiercely resisted, even by peasants with very small holdings. Land-ownership is deeply ingrained, and is felt to be a right, one which has commonly extended over generations. Beyond this, great land-owners have been ready to use their privately recruited strong-arm gangs to increase their ownership by dispossessing the local peasantry or tribal communities. This has involved violent intimidation, and even murder.

Against such a background it would be naive to expect a co-operative to improve things for the local peasantry. Its initiatives would simply be swept out of existence. Any lawyer who pleads for this is likely to be intimidated, assaulted, even killed. Nevertheless, there are some lawyers who are astute, experienced and courageous, and will speak; but such are likely to be heavily over-loaded.

Pearse and Stiefel identify several agencies which will oppose themselves to participatory developments. These include bureaucracies; industrial enterprises based on advanced technologies; complex urban-centred economic, political and social systems (eg education?) One would add the military, the police and church hierarchies, even though, at the present time, churches are often ready to speak with two voices. Pearse and Stiefel are right to put first *"ideologies created by dominant classes to maintain existing monopolies and forms of exploitation."* Their term is *"structures of anti-participation"*: they observe that even institutions set up to promote the participation of the many often become instruments operated by the few in their own interests.

There can be little doubt that the U.N.R.I.S.D. analysis is also relevant for the over-developed countries, where violence is muted and alienation is rewarded.

A general conclusion would be that small co-operatives will be ignored, and larger ones tolerated up to a point. That point will be the moment when co-operatives are numerous enough, and large enough, to constitute a critical mass, and to demonstrate an alternative mode of life, work and public administration. We may predict that they will then be subjected to legal, economic and fiscal constraints sufficient to cripple them - as will be the case with any movement which brings benefit to the many at some cost to the rich and powerful in control of most of our industrial/financial governmental institutions.

"Conflictive participation" will prove to be an appropriate concept in both advanced and developing countries.

Co-operative Credit Unions

In countries rich and poor there are money-lenders. They charge very high rates of interest, commonly more than 100% per annum, for lending to the poor who, so often, desperately need money for emergencies. In Britain, where 30,000 people are said to die of cold in their own houses every year, the need may be to pay an electricity bill, or it may be for children's food and school clothes, following on reductions in welfare payments. Such people are not credit-worthy to the banks. However, dozens of retailing chains have given them credit cards, against which they have accumulated large debts. The dread of foreclosure, eviction and the reality of a cut-off of the gas and electricity supply hangs over them. They may indeed have been poor managers; the financial pages of our newspapers tell us every day that earners of high incomes may also be bad managers. To people in such a predicament, the tally-man, or loan shark to use the newspaper term, comes as a saviour. Of course, his ministrations ensure a tightening of the noose a little later.

There is a co-operative alternative; the local credit union. It is run by local people, who understand all the pressure points and will offer support and advice. It invites the debt-trapped citizen into membership. Against small regular payments, it will lend money at minimal interest rates, sometimes as low as 2%. It is staffed by volunteers and operates with a capital of a few thousand pounds.

In India, credit co-operatives have been set up to help poor farmers over the growing season until their meagre crop is ready. How will the village money-lender view this development? At a blow, it could rob him of most of his income and his traditional status in local life. It can be no surprise that he will sometimes conspire with the local landowner to block the operation of such a scheme. Intimidation will, usually, be enough: the threat of loss of part-time employment as a day labourer, or access to the landlord's water pump. Sometimes, strong-arm methods will be used, meetings disrupted. How will the money-lending agencies respond to the steady growth of credit unions in Britain? What happens when their national organisation achieves substance and scale? For what purpose was the co-operative banking facility established in Rochdale 1844, and what happened to it? What has been the history of the Trustee Savings Bank? Presumably, they could have addressed themselves towards those most in need of credit. But that would not have been commercial; so they were assimilated.

In 1988, there were 150 credit unions in Britain. By 1993, numbers had increased to 400, and are expected to reach 600 by 1995. They do not necessarily address those in greatest need. It is a perfectly feasible model for the needs of well-paid staff. Further developments are awaited.

The Question of Scale

The Industrial Common Ownership Movement reports that, in 1982-3, central government support to private sector industry amounted to £54 billion. Support for co-operatives, under the Inner Urban Areas Act and channelled through local authorities, was estimated at £3 million. So, for every £1 to the co-operatives, private enterprise received £18,000. If that ratio were reversed, over a period, the entire socio-economic scene might well be transformed. Most of the support for co-operatives went towards small-scale start-up enterprise, with some intention to provide work for unemployed and disadvantaged people. Although thousands of co-operatives were created, the overall effect has been a reduction in average size, which tends towards further marginalisation.

If co-operatives are to establish themselves among the large corporations at the centre of the economy, this will come about by rescue operations based on employee ownership. The evidence is that these can be successful, even highly successful. Presumably, the £54 billion for the private sector included huge appropriations for British Leyland, Harland and Wolf, some aerospace projects, nuclear power, in all of which vast debts had to be written off. Much better prospects for a good return on public money would have resulted from making loans for worker buy-outs in other sectors. This is a political issue; and everyone recognises that military requirements have determined investments in aero-space and nuclear power.

The questions of scale have been approached too much in structural terms. The phenomena of group life exhibit regularities which bear little relation to group size. This, at least, seems to have been the view of the pioneering scholars who have investigated group life. Le Bon McDougall, concluded that numbers were not the prime factor in the formation of the group mind. Freud endorsed this conclusion. His focus on the modes of relating to the leader, and to fellow-members, had reference to the family, the primal horde and, surprisingly, to great social institutions, notably the church and the army. Bion, the most influential psycho-analytical group therapist, followed Freud's example in this, while basing his interpretation on the postulates of Melanie Klein and on phenomenology. Like Freud, he moves easily from his observations of groups to interpretations of behaviour in large national systems. Everyday speech recognises the concepts of leadership and morale as applicable to small groups, large systems and whole nations. The key factor appears to be the extent to which people recognise themselves as a group having collective interests, an identity, perhaps a name and a history — however sketchy or legendary; and of course a leader, alive or dead, or even abstract. Group size was not a major factor. Reference has been made to the use of groups in the revelation of the social dynamics of national, and even international, systems by setting up mini-economies with exchange simulations, class structures and regulatory institutions.

We have argued that Periclean Athens was the super-nova of our civilisation, in which the elements and the atomic units of our later thought systems were forged. Many have called attention to the small scale of the Athenian city state, relative to the huge scale of later nation-states. But Athens could equally be seen as a very large group. It was small enough for most of its influential citizens to know each other in some personal sense, not exclusively as with the early Eupatrids, but with an openness to common citizens in the street and in the assembly. Does this point on the scale between a very large group and a very small nation suggest a critical mass within which some kind of chain reaction becomes probable?

Chapter Seven

Collective Responsibility, Learning and the Quality of Life

In the State of to-day, in which democratic control through Parliament is little better than a farce, the Collectivist State would be the Earthly Paradise of bureaucracy.

The Socialist, in most cases, admits this but declares that it could be corrected if Parliament were democratised. The "conquest of political power" becomes the Alpha and Omega of his political method: all his cheques are post-dated to the Greek Kalends of the first Socialist Government ... The postal workers are no more free while the Post Office is managed by a State department than Trade Unionists would be free if their Executive Committees were appointed by His Majesty's Minister of Labour. (**Self-Government in Industry**: G.D.H. Cole, 1971, Hutchinson, pp.43/44.)

Scott Bader

Scott Bader has been the best-known co-operative enterprise in Britain during the twentieth century (but discounting the great C.W.S). It has been in business for 72 years, and became a co-operative Commonwealth in 1951. Its main product is a thermo-setting polyester which has a wide variety of uses. Current turn-over exceeds £45 million, with profits of £2,900,000 per annum. There are more than 400 worker members. The record is one of steady growth.

Severyn T. Bruyn tells the story of the Scott Bader Commonwealth in his *Quaker Testimonies and Economic Alternatives,* a Pendle Hill Pamphlet from Pennsylvania, 1980, in the chapter headed Quaker Experiments with Common Ownership.

It *"was organized formally to reflect the principles embodied in the socialist tradition of Robert Owen and the religious tradition of Friends"* and membership was open to all employees after a probationary period. The General Meeting, its main legislative body, met quarterly *"to review the general conduct of the business"* and *"its power included the right to approve large investments before they were made, and to dispose of the profits recommended by the Community Council"* — the main administrative body — *"and the Board of Directors."* The Community Council was composed of nine people elected by the membership, two nominated by the Board and one representing the local community — 12 people in all.

All members were equal, with one vote at the General Meeting, and all employees *"became salaried and were given a greater income equity than is customary in the orthodox firm."* There was also a high degree of job security, with a representative appeal system available to any employee.

It is claimed that more than 1,000 companies have since followed the Scott-Bader model. Fritz Schumacher was one of its early directors. His experience may well have influenced his thinking in *"Small is Beautiful"*.

> *His ideas have had a profound and lasting effect over the last 25 years. They helped form the ideological basis for the "Green" parties, with their support for small-scale enterprises producing for social need, and their commitment to ensuring that workers have more control over their lives.* (No Single Model, I.C.O.M., 1987).

Schumacher's Intermediate Technology was largely funded by the Commonwealth.

Scott Bader also originated I.C.O.M — the Industrial Common Ownership Movement — which has since received support from other sources and publishes a range of useful informative and practical booklets, many of which are oriented towards small and start-up enterprise. It is somewhat surprising to find that in presenting their case studies of larger co-operatives they choose four with 17, 179 (including part-timers), 20 and 27 worker/members. This was appropriate in addressing the problems of growth beyond the face-to-face group. They write: *"it is clear, however, that co-operatives must get away from the rigid trap of consensus if they are going to grow and succeed. Once the work-force numbers over twenty, the structure of the co-operative must change if it is to survive."* (p.20)

Scott Bader was already in a different league when it was endowed, having then 150 members. It was an ethical motive that led Ernest Bader to endow the Commonwealth in 1951, by simply giving to it 90% of his shares. This not-quite-complete gift *"created tensions"*, and the remaining 10% were given in 1963. A new employee may apply for membership of the Commonwealth after 18 months, when he must agree to support the Constitution and Code of Practice, which embodies the following ethical aims:

- mutual responsibility;
- rendering the best possible service as a corporate body to our fellow men;
- producing goods beneficial to the community;
- providing fair conditions;
- job and wealth sharing;
- democratic involvement and accountability;
- management by consent and not by coercion;
- responsible management of the earth's resources.

These aims are based ethically, and in practice, on the belief that people are more important than money and capital. Therefore members work within a democratic self-governing structure, and are expected to contribute to the wholeness of the community, both materially, spiritually and in the quality of their relationships, together. All are equal members within the Commonwealth, with one vote, irrespective of their position in the Company. Ratification of major policies after discussion is carried out at general meetings, by members voting on proposals presented by the Board of the Scott Bader Operating Company.

There is a commitment to full employment, in that all members agree to accept reduced pay in difficult times, rather than that anyone should be made redundant. There is also a strong environmental consciousness.

They further state that *"power should come from within the person and the community and be made responsible to those it affects"* and that human dignity and service to others should be the ultimate criteria in work organisation — not just economic performance. Mutual responsibility, supported by democratic participation and the principle of trusteeship, should permeate the whole community of work:

> *Common-ownership of our means of production, and a voice in the distribution of earned surplus and the allocation of new capital, has helped us in our struggle towards achieving these aims.*

It is claimed that the Commonwealth is endeavouring to fulfil its responsibilities to the wider national and international community by *"fostering a movement towards a new peaceful industrial and social order"*, which, in order to be a genuine alternative to welfare capitalism and state-controlled communism, *"must be non-violent in the sense of promoting love and justice, for where love stops, power begins and intimidation and violence follow."* Organisation of work, based on these principles, is, they assert, *"one of the main requirements of a peaceful social order"*, together with sharing with the less fortunate and refusing *"to support destructive social conflict or to take part in preparations for war."*

In a more recent statement on the environment, they affirm their commitment to the use of *"the best practicable means available to achieve a better environment"*, which they have endeavoured to implement by investing *"considerable sums of money"* in plans and equipment" to minimise the impact of their activities. Environmental aspects, such as noise pollution, air pollution, water pollution, land pollution are considered, *"with careful monitoring both on and off site."* Representatives of the following enforcement agencies ensure that they adhere to statutory requirements in dealing with these matters: The Industrial Air Pollution Inspectorate, the Environmental Health Department, the Hazardous Waste Inspectorate, the Anglian Water Authority, the Health and Safety Executive, Specialist Groups, General Factory Inspectors and Northamptonshire County Council.

Schumacher fathered the phrase *"small is beautiful"*, which he saw as applying to technology, ethnicity, ecology and social organisation. Much as he valued small co-operatives, it is not clear that he wanted them to be as small as possible. No doubt he influenced Scott Bader in limiting the Commonwealth to 450 members, when the outlook was promising, and members could have enriched themselves by adopting a policy of continuous growth. It appears that small co-operatives provide a very real, if strenuous and anxious, experience for their members, leaving them disinclined to take on the demands of growth. If the growth process is accepted, there may be no clear indication of having reached the point of arrest. Perhaps the Scott Bader limit was arbitrary; or if it was rational, it was based on values rather than economic rationality.

It is clear that the appeal is to human values, and to daily experience at a basic level. Security is indeed a basic consideration in a world of economic disorder and constantly rising unemployment. The knowledge that one's colleagues will not impose redundancy if one's skill is outmoded by technological developments; that the chance to learn new skills and so to make one's contribution will be provided. Security of that kind is indeed basic to one's view of life itself. It invokes trust, reciprocity and fellow-feeling. Inseparable from such basic certainty is personal commitment and responsibility. These are binding on the co-operator from the first moment. Furthermore, the commitment requires that each member shall learn by doing and by listening, and that such learning shall entail careful consideration about what shall be done. It will soon be clear that deep issues are implicated in many decisions, decisions so often elided where a simple competitive rationale prevails.

It is clear from all that has been said that the practice of co-operation can enhance the quality of life of each person who commits himself to it. The learning by experience that is entailed is vastly greater than that available to the worker in a private firm. Indeed, the principle has been proposed in a school of management that an employed person should not be trained beyond the requirements of his/her task, because it may result in discontent, frustrated ambition or union activism. This is a formula for producing an alienated, unco-operative and uncreative work-force. Collective responsibility demands the exact opposite. A citation from Stern's report for the EEC will illustrate the point:

> *It emerges from this study that co-operation can be very different from conventional enterprises, for example:*
> - *in the reported job satisfaction of both workers and managers;*
> - *in the job security they offer employees in comparison with other firms in their sector;*
> - *in their limited hierarchies and high levels of trust between employees;*
> - *in their commitment to consensus management and good conditions of employment; and*
> - *in their capacity to innovate and respond flexibly to uncertain market conditions.* (p.57)

In the Context of Education

Formal education has been with us for perhaps three thousand years. There is a distinguished literature, extending over more than two thousand: Plato, Quintilian, Cicero, St Augustine, Erasmus, Comenius, Pestalozzi, Rousseau, Locke, Steiner, Mill, William James, Spencer, Whitehead, Herbert Read, J.H. Newman are only a few who made valued contributions.

By contrast, the history of education as practised, at least up to the second world war, makes dismal, even horrifying, reading; partly because of the squalor of most of the available schools, the ignorance of the largely unqualified teachers, and mostly because of the generally sanctioned savage punishments administered, and the tolerated brutality from child to child. Behind this was the centrality of Latin, even centuries after it had lost its use as a medium for international scholarship.

While noting, with E.M. Forster, that on reading a few pages of a Tolstoy novel, one soon begins to *"hear the deep chords sounding"*, in Tolstoy's work on education one is impressed by his great concentration on teaching as a very human task. It was a serious concern for him. He travelled extensively in Germany, France and England for the express purpose of studying schools and learning about the best practice. He found almost all of them abysmally bad by his own standards. He returned to his own estate at Yasnaya, founded and personally taught at a school for peasant children. His methods were widely adopted, and there were soon thirteen village schools in the district. Inevitably, his philosophy, which steadily converged upon a form of Christian anarchism, was unacceptable to the rulers of Russia — then, and now, it seems. His publications were suppressed and his influence on the education system was extinguished. But the record remains, a trumpet-call to all teachers with a basic human concern for their pupils.

He wrote

> *... in spite of the preponderating influence of the teacher, the pupil has always had the right not to come to school, or, having come, not to listen to the teacher. The teacher has had the right not to admit a pupil, and has had the possibility of bringing to bear all the force of his influence on the majority of pupils, on the society, always composed of the school children.*

Some adults chose to attend in the evenings, and committed themselves to the development of literacy skills.

Tolstoy's schools were not examples of self-government, but they certainly manifested the principle of freedom; the freedom of teachers to programme themselves and to teach what they could teach best; the freedom of children to come and go as they pleased, and to take some responsibility for collective discipline; the freedom of peasants and parents to send or withdraw their children, or themselves to share in the learning process — some became literate that way. Such freedom is basic to anarchist thinking.

The Great Democrat

Now let us give credit where it is due: to A. S. Neill — his life work, his practice, his humour and his values, unquestionably based on his delight in children.

As a Scottish dominie, Neill was sickened and revolted by the rigidities and cruelties of the system in which he taught. He left it, and eventually established Summerhill, of international fame, largely based on his observation of Homer Lane's work with young delinquents at the Little Commonwealth, for which he had a deep respect. He attracted enough pupils, many from overseas, to survive, though in straitened financial circumstances. He regretted his dependence on the patronage of rich parents. Other pioneers have worked with state-supported children, notable David Wills, quaker, with disturbed children, and E. F. O'Neill who, after some rugged experiences in and out of teaching, was finally allowed to run (successfully) a state secondary school in industrial Lancashire on equally original principles. It was supported by senior H.M.I.s and visited by coach-loads of educationists, (including the present writer).

Neill's principles centred upon the abrogation of authority (though not of responsibility) by the adults — teachers, head and ancillary staff. It follows that they could not, and did not, attempt to impose discipline or punishment. A collective discipline emerged, and the nature of it has been significant for our argument.

Neill found that the children, given total freedom, without exception opted to attend lessons, usually within the first three weeks. If any child became a nuisance in the classroom, the others would tell him or her to quieten down, or get out: keeping order did not fall to the teacher alone.

The school was governed by general meetings of children, staff and ancillaries, everyone equal in that each had one vote, and could speak freely on all issues. Staff were frequently out-voted. School rules had to be collectively determined and infractions of them penalised. The participation of staff and the willingness to talk through all issues obviated the danger of relapse into a Lord-of-the-Flies situation.

The school assembly fell into every predictable kind of difficulty, one of which is a universal: apathy, non-participation, indifference to democratic rights, lapses in attendance. If it appeared that the collective was failing to accept its responsibilities, Neill would arbitrarily abolish it, and declare himself a dictator — this in the 1930s. The children and, no doubt, the staff, fully accustomed to personal autonomy, would call the meeting together and vote Neill of out office.

Such developments are comic, but profoundly educative. At a conference, in the 1960s, of workers with disturbed or delinquent adolescents, one in charge of a residential home reported his experience of such collective responsibility. He said that, due to problems of violence and general destructiveness, often in the form of open conflict between rival groups struggling for power and dominance, the home had been closed three times. He expressed no intention of changing the method, nor even any sense of disillusion. Living through such turbulent experiences of participation could be a great learning experience for young people. It will have left in them some real understanding of social claims on individual behaviour.

Neill may stand as the greatest educationist in British history. His reputation was international — his work was more recognised abroad than in Britain: a not unfamiliar situation. It is of the highest relevance for us today; but the reader must recognise the historical context. Neill's fulminations against moralistic religious teaching and the attempted total repression of sexuality in children are much less relevant today.

Our concern is with self-managing systems. In his book, Summerhill, Neill gives a vivid account of self-government as practised in his school. He explains the democratic principles on which the school is run, with each member of the community, teachers and pupils alike (including Neill himself) having one vote at the Saturday night General School Meeting and with all votes carrying equal weight, from those of seven-year-olds to his own vote. At this meeting, *"Everything connected with social, or group, life, including punishment for social offences, is settled by vote."* He then makes the interesting comment that *"No culprit at Summerhill ever shows any signs of defiance or hatred of the authority of his community. I am always surprised at the docility our pupils show when punished"*, and illustrates this remark by telling of the occasion when four of the biggest boys had broken the rule which forbids the sale of articles from their wardrobes — a law which *"had been passed on the ground that such practices are unfair to the parents who buy the clothes and unfair as well to the school, because when children go home minus certain wearing apparel, the parents blame the school for carelessness."* The boys' punishment was *"being kept on the grounds for four days and being sent to bed at eight each night"*, a sentence they completely accepted, to the extent that, on a night when everyone had gone to the cinema, Neill asked one of the culprits, who was in bed reading, why he did not get up, only to receive the reply *"Don't try to be funny."*

Neill describes the pupils' loyalty to their own democracy as amazing, being devoid of both fear and resentment, and tells us that it often happens that a boy who has undergone a long trial and been sentenced for *"some antisocial act"*, is elected chairman for the next meeting. He goes on to make the illuminating comment: *"The sense of justice that children have never ceases to make me marvel. And their administrative ability is great. As education, self-government is of infinite value."*

It seems that the only occasion Neill could remember, on which the meeting had sought an adult's advice, was when three girls who had raided the kitchen larder were, firstly, fined their pocket money and then, when they repeated the offence, fined a cinema visit. This still did not deter them from offending again and the meeting was *"gravelled what to do"*. When the chairman sought Neill's advice, the latter suggested giving the girls a reward of tuppence and the chairman's scandalised reply was: *"What? Why, man, you'll have the whole school raiding the kitchen if we do that"*, whereupon Neill again advised him to try it, which he did. The result was that *"Two of the girls refused to take the money; and all three were heard to declare that they would never raid the larder again. They didn't — for about two months."*

He goes on to describe the lack of bureaucracy at Summerhill: *"The secretary's job is voluntary. Bedtime officers are seldom in office for more than a few weeks."* He informs us that there were good laws made by their democracy, such as sea-bathing being forbidden without supervision by staff, acting as life-guards; climbing on roofs was not allowed; bedtimes had to be kept; a vote was taken before each holiday, to decide whether classes should be called off on the Thursday or on the Friday preceding the holiday. As one might expect, we are told that *"The success of the meeting depends largely on whether the chairman is weak or strong, for to keep order among forty-five vigorous children is no easy task. The chairman has power to fine noisy citizens. Under a weak chairman, the fines are much too frequent."*

The aspects of the life of the school which were not subject to self-government were such matters as the appointment and dismissal of teachers, which were done by Neill himself, and bedroom arrangements, menus and financial matters, which were dealt with by Mrs Neill.

Neill points out that their self-government entails social features, as well as law-making. Every term starts with rules about bedtime being made: *"You go to bed according to your age",* followed by questions of general behaviour, the election of sports committees, *"an end-of-term dance committee, a theatre committee, bedtime officers, and downtown officers who report any disgraceful behaviour out of the school boundaries."* Neill tells us that he never felt the need to alter his views on self- government; it was their showpiece and he could not visualise Summerhill without it. It seems it has its drawbacks, however, at times when a delicate matter such as the blocking of toilets by sanitary towels has to be brought up at a meeting when visitors are present.

One final paragraph sums up his philosophy:

> *The educational benefit of practical civics cannot be over-emphasized. At Summerhill, the pupils would fight to the death for their right to govern themselves. In my opinion, one weekly General School Meeting is of more value than a week's curriculum of school subjects. It is an excellent theatre for practising public speaking, and most of the children speak well and without self-consciousness. I have often heard sensible speeches from children who could neither read nor write.*

The foregoing chapters on Periclean Athens, on the Kibbutzim and on quality of life in producer co-operatives, have emphasised self-management in the formation of persons and in essential learning.

Summerhill was subjected to a full inspection by H.M.I in 1949. The report is included in the **Summerhill** book, pp.77-86. They recognised at the start that *"This School is famous throughout the world"* for its revolutionary practice. They give a detailed and sympathetic account of what they observed. They also recognise that Neill would feel that:

> *... his school must stand or fall rather by the kind of children that it allows its pupils to grow into, than by the specific skills and abilities that it teaches them. On the basis of evaluation it may be said:*
>
> *1. That the children are full of life and zest. Of boredom and apathy there was no sign. An atmosphere of contentment and tolerance pervades the school ...*
>
> *2. That the children's manners are delightful ... their total lack of shyness and self-consciousness, their friendliness, ease and naturalness made them very easy, pleasant people to get on with ...*

Following Neill's death, the school was taken over by his daughter. It continues in being after more than 70 years.

In Higher Education

Self-responsibility in higher learning, and especially in training for "people work", as in counselling and therapy, social and community work is becoming the norm — although collective responsibility has been more difficult to actualise.

No-one has questioned the claim that shared responsibility enhances the development of the person. It calls all faculties into play, even when processes involved are time-consuming, difficult and sometimes painful. It is the royal road towards learning and quality of life. In 1970, a new community and Youth Work course was started at the University of London, Goldsmiths College. A feature which was novel at the time was the regular term-time Friday morning meetings of the entire department: students, teaching staff, office staff and any others. Items for the agenda were invited; any person or group could raise any question or make proposals. Differences in status and responsibility were not denied; Dr Josephine Klein, course director, made clear that she would reserve for herself the decision on many matters under discussion. The total openness between staff and students on such concerns as assessment, selection, course attendance, or report writing was innovative. An observer wrote:

> *The course encourages the ongoing learning process by developing levels of consciousness, personal confidence and skills in human relationships. This is achieved by not imposing the constraints of conventional teaching methods which seek to direct students into consciously labelled and set teaching periods, eg, compulsory or semi-compulsory lectures.*

When left to themselves, how many people participate in community work projects? How many people make constructive criticisms rather than voting with their feet? How can students forced to attend lectures learn to deal with these realities if they are not experiencing the problems for themselves in themselves?

They regard this difficult experience as central to the ongoing learning process of the student. This can mystify, anger, upset, disappoint, confuse students.

It worked well, and somewhat similar developments were later observed in other courses.

This is not an example of direct democracy, as final decisions were reserved. The great freedom of speech, however, brought with it the ethos of democracy. It appears in many historical examples that the felt need is for such freedom of speech and self-expression in itself, generating some acceptance that if the decision-makers are willing to listen, to give their time and attention to what is being said, the outcome may be more satisfactory than if the whole group, the people, were required to determine issues of which their understanding is limited.

Forms of democracy may be imposed by authority, without the option. Many examples cited in this text started that way and then lifted off into their own orbit. It is surprising to observe how many, once a form had been worked out with a dominant leader, subsequently adhered to it without modification. The continuing importance of the departed leader is well recognised in group analysis.

In the 1930s and 1940s, the German people had some experience of *Demokratie* but much more of *Diktatur*. When the Allies imposed their own representative systems, with little consultation, the Germans called it *Demokratur*. That was an apt name, perhaps even a concept.

Academics have been indifferent to their democratic rights. They seem to be somewhat relieved if other people are willing to take on the running of the department in which they teach. One could observe in one university, following the student upheavals of 1968/69, when universities were paralysed by the occupation by students of their administrative offices, it was thought appropriate to have a student representation on Senate, the ruling academic body. Career-grade non-professorial staff found themselves outflanked. This was because they had complacently allowed power and policy-making to remain with the professors. An increase in their representation did little to remedy that situation.

The beginnings of a direct democracy, however, by the establishment of Departmental Boards did have an effect. They were commonly chaired by members of lecturer grade; collective views were expressed which, as some statutes said, it would have been unwise for appointed heads of departments to ignore. Perhaps the main change was a new openness of information, particularly on finance. Such information had not been formally withheld: it was a matter of bringing it into general circulation. In some cases, it was open to students to attend and, sometimes to speak. Usually, they were bored.

They were not the only ones to be bored by meetings based on long and detailed agendas. Staff members became lax in attendance: at least, this was true in some cases.

If staff members do not participate, then the necessary decisions will be made by their superiors in status, and less openly. This neglect may result in considerable damage to their own interests. Most lecturers were outraged by the legislation of 1988, which robbed them of tenure and, therefore, of academic freedom; which proposed to subordinate and re-structure universities in accordance with the prevailing party political view of the national interest. If there had been a practice of full and responsible participation by all teaching staff, a solidarity might well have emerged, with a refusal to implement a whole range of imposed decisions. As it is, we observe late in the day a department making mandatory the participation of all staff members at its board meetings, on penalty of submitting an explanatory letter in case of default.

Autonomy

Stone clearly demonstrates the association between the continuing creativity of Athens and its generally prevailing freedom of expression; with its sustained reputation as a university city through the centuries of the Roman empire, and with the duration of the Academy (Plato) and the Lyceum (Aristotle); and with its overwhelming creative brilliance during the two centuries of participatory democracy. That was the historic moment when, as a minute embryo, the processes of intellectual growth and differentiation began which have now attained to such scale and such power as to overwhelm us in our time, unless we achieve some collective coherence in the face of our extraordinary contemporary situation.

Stone regards freedom of speech as the basic socio-political value. What then is the relation between freedom of speech, freedom of thought and democracy? Psychologists and anthropologists have examined the relation between speech, language and thought. For instance, can deaf-mutes, who are likely to remain illiterate be capable of conceptual thinking? Given that the answer is positive, we may still assert that socially and culturally, language and thought are reciprocally inter-dependent. Cultural development has increasingly depended upon the written word, and in recent centuries on printing. The freedoms of thought, speech and publication are seen to be inseparable. Long-term suppression of certain proscribed ideological or literary content has affected collective thinking over generations.

The question that remains concerns the relations between freedom of speech, freedom of publication and democracy. The ideal type will simply assert that democracy is directly and wholly dependent on freedom of speech and publication. Development theory, both Marxian and liberal, has assumed that where such freedoms can be brought about, a collective demand for participation in decision-making political processes will be generated. Historians, who are necessarily disinclined to accede to general assumptions, may be content to state that in the histories of all nations all freedoms have been partial, that the outcomes can never be understood in unitary causality and that all is relative. To this we may assent, and we would lay stress upon the conclusion that all democracies so far have been very limited, even the best of them. In our time we may be tempted to think that the more democracy is claimed and proclaimed in the West, the more fraudulent it appears.

The rights of women, and of slaves, may be relativised by a consideration of the rights of children. In Rome the *patria potestas* gave to the father the legal right of life and death over his children. In East Africa recently relief workers were surprised to receive some families which had trekked long distances to the refugee camp in conditions of near starvation, and to find young children at the point of death while the parents had fed themselves reasonably well. The parents explained their choice in these terms: If we fed the children and starved ourselves, then we would all die. If the children die, that is not so bad. When the food situation improves we can get some more children. In classical times also, the question as to whether to raise one's children or not might be seen as an arbitrary matter, related to overall circumstances. In our time, the media inform us of cruelties imposed on children beyond the imagination of the normal citizen. That citizen may equally be astonished to read of a recent Swedish enactment to the effect that no child is ever to be hit. This means that no parent is ever to punish his/her own child by physical means. "Astonished" may be too mild a term; "astounded" might truly denote the response of those who over the millennia from Solomon onwards have been enjoined not to spare the rod or strap, and have endlessly been advised that the systematic beating of the children is their first duty. How have the Scottish dominies, reluctant to forego the use of the tawse, reacted? Yet there can be little doubt that the Swedish initiative will be followed. We may expect that in the course of time it will be embodied in the Universal Declaration of Human Rights. A. S. Neill's impassioned condemnation of the beating of children does honour to his memory, though he was not alone in this. That was sixty years ago. A hundred years ago the debate turned on whether and in what circumstances men could beat their wives.

From this we may draw two main pointers in the assessment of Athenian practice in respect of human rights, or that of any society. First, while the practice may be judged against a scale of universal values, it is to be understood in historical and comparative terms. Second is the recognition that all cultural systems in the modern world are gravely defective in respect of the rights of women, children; and oppressed peoples and classes. Slavery has not been eliminated; it may be increasing.

Chapter Eight

Anarchism: Theory and Practice

In 1983 Ricardo Semler published his account of the successful revolution he had instituted in a Brazilian manufacturing company. This involved:

1. Shedding seven layers of management;
2. Permitting all employees to set their own hours of work;
3. Permitting all employees to choose their own place of work (e.g. home);
4. Permitting all employees to fix their own salary scales;
5. Permitting all employees to rate their own bosses as managers;
6. Permitting all employees to decide allocation of surpluses to investment etc.

Productivity has increased seven-fold, profits five-fold, to nearly $3 million, from 200 workers.

Semler thinks of himself as introducing democracy to the firm. Certainly the degree of individual responsibility and collective decision-making parallels that of the best co-operatives on record. There is something more, however. The wholesale abolition of tiers of management and the relaxation of clock time as the operational framework transcend the concepts of representative democracy. It is, without recognizing itself, a variety of anarchism.

There could be an element of comedy in delegates from the great co-operatives visiting Semco, to see what they can learn. It is, of course, quite impossible for them to learn. They must resemble visitors to the early zoos who, having refused to believe the illustrations in the natural history books, still could not accept the existence of a giraffe, even after seeing one. The whole set-up must appear to them unrealistic; difficult to realise; yet it exists in reality. It is true for us all that what we see as real is no more than a narrow arrow-slit view of a vast landscape.

Even if this brilliant initiative, like many before it, slowly reverts to a more conventional mode, it will always remain as an historic example, an episode of profound significance.

Anarchism has had a long and distinguished history, extending over more than 200 years, Godwin and Shelley inspired their literary friends before the French revolution. Coleridge and, no doubt, Wordsworth, nourished expectations that, when the peasant populations of Europe broke free from the great structures of privilege and control under which they lived, they would produce and exchange what they produced, freely and with benefit to all. Great names that have contributed to the Anarchist literature in the nineteenth century included Emerson, Thoreau, Tolstoy, Stirner, Proudhon, Bakunin, Malatesta, Kroptokin; and, in this century, Herbert Read, Alex Comfort and the two great expositors, Colin Ward and George Woodcock. The Anarchist doctrines have been strongest in Spain and Italy and have given rise to some spectacular initiatives.

A libertarian poster of our time proclaims: *"There's no government like no government."* That is probably how most people think of anarchism and it is not a bad starting point. It presents a challenge, requires us to examine every article of government and to question how far, under close scrutiny, it can be proved beneficial. The question is never easy to answer. Point by point, such a scrutiny reveals vast complex interlocking systems, enterprises and agencies, demanding huge resources; and failing to meet elementary needs. The most powerful quantitative analyses have been those of Ivan Illich, showing that education, medicine, transport, make worse the conditions — ignorance, sickness, spatial constraints — they are established to relieve. No equivalent rebuttals of Illich's cases have appeared during ten years. The list of such failures could be extended: the prison system, psychotherapy, housing, welfare, control of crime. In each case, the picture that emerges is of an educated bureaucracy, heavily overloaded and failing to cope with rising needs.

Probably few anarchists envisage a large society with no central government, though some would not rule it out as a long-term possibility. George Woodcock cites Emerson, who was not, in fact, a committed anarchist:

> *Every actual State is corrupt. Good men must not obey the laws too well ... Wild liberty develops iron conscience. Want of liberty, by strengthening law and decorum, stupefies conscience.*

and Thoreau:

> *I heartily accept the motto — 'That government is best which governs least'; and I should like to see it acted up to more rapidly and system-*

atically. Carried out it finally amounts to this, which I also believe — 'That government is best which governs not at all', and when men are prepared for it, that will be the kind of government which they will have. Government is at best but an expedient; but most governments are usually, and all governments are sometimes, inexpedient. (Wooodcock, p.429)

Kropotkin states:

A great part of that order which reigns among mankind is not the effect of government. It has its origins in the principles of society and the natural constitution of men. It existed prior to government and would exist if the formality of government were abolished. The mutual dependence and reciprocal interest which man has upon man, and all the parts of civilised community upon each other, create that great chain of connection which holds it together.

Kropotkin was able to draw on the mass of anthropological material already available for his great anarchist text **Mutual Aid,** 1902. His project was to document mutual aid as *"a law of nature and chief factor of progressive evolution."* This was to negate the grossly unwarranted appropriation of Darwin's all-against-all model of natural selection for the legitimation of rampant capitalist competition as the sole factor in economic development. Raymond Williams powerfully exposed this misappropriation.

I have already commented in my monograph **Ideologies,** pp.8/9: the unwillingness of conservative and liberal philosophers to recognise that the activity of powerful industrial commercial entities led to the crudest form of liberal conservatism, which is sometimes called Social Darwinism. This flourished in the later part of the last century. Darwin's immense impact on public consciousness was found useful by the large units of a freely competitive system. The *"survival of the fittest"* — Herbert Spencer's phrase — was taken over; the assumption was made that businesses, governments or nations which survived were those that were most fitted to survive — so that success and power were self-justifying. There was no recognition that the natural kingdom which Darwin studied offered abundant examples of successfully surviving parasites, disease organisms, carnivores, or creatures inhabiting narrow cracks in the ecological system which afforded them a toe-hold on existence. I take some examples from Raymond Williams: Spencer opposed state aid to the poor on the grounds that this would preserve the weaker members of the race. He thought, and many of the elite Victorians did, that it was their duty to have large families while the poor should be discouraged from that, or their children should at least not be maintained. *"Artificial preservation"* was a mistake — it was necessary that such people should die: whereas millionaires, said Sumner, another sociologist, are a product of natural selection. Rockefeller said the growth of a large business is merely the survival of the fittest. In Germany, von Moltke argued for war, saying that only the strongest survive it, and only they can ensure the future of humanity. The argument was carried further to justify the existence of the British empire and its disregard of the rights of the weaker races. The dominance of the United States in economic and commercial terms was justified as the effectiveness of a more vigorous anglo-saxon hybrid stock (on the biological analogy that hybrid stocks are more vigorous). Of course, the argument of the survival of the fittest was used by the Nazis. W.A. Mallock used it against the extension of education — he said that if you extended education, it could only result in articulate mass democracy acting as a drag upon the necessary actions of a great leader, who must emerge by competition. All this despite the arguments of the excellent T.H. Huxley, who said the whole confusion had arisen from identifying the fittest with the best, or of Kropotkin, who showed that in nature competition between species occurs, whereas within the species behaviour was frequently co-operative; and of Darwin himself, who complained that he had been represented as proving that might is right — that Napoleon was right and that every cheating tradesmen was right. Nevertheless, the fantasy that general benefits would result from the destruction of weak social units by strong ones was sedulously and successfully disseminated. The Marxist concept of ideology would explain that as a way of seeing the world, a way of seeing the social system, propagated by controlling elites who have an interest in its acceptance as reality and as common sense.

Of **Mutual Aid,** Alex Comfort has written:

> *The earliest theorists of anarchism, such as William Godwin and Kropotkin, strikingly anticipate the findings of sociology in their estimate of human behaviour and the means of modifying conduct ... Kropotkin profoundly influenced human biology by his theory of Mutual Aid, propounded as a counterblast to the social conclusions drawn from the Darwinian struggle for existence. He was one of the first systematic students of animal communities, and may be regarded as the founder of modern social ecology.*

The most assiduous writer on anarchism over the last two decades has been Colin Ward. Perhaps his work will now attract the greater recognition it deserves as a third way is increasingly sought as a positive alternative to unbridled capitalism on the one hand and a centralised Leninist/Marxism on the other. In his introduction to Kropotkin's **Fields, Factories and Workshops Tomorrow** — he writes:

> *How on earth has the socialist movement got itself into the position of dismissing as petit-bourgeois individualism all those freedoms which people actually value: everything belongs to the private dreams that people really cherish?*

This is an important question, and as I stress in my original introduction, Kropotkin's contribution to all our private dreams is that it is a thesis on the economic consequence of the humanisation of work.

Josiah Warren

It is possible that most people find the anarchist project simply incredible. By way of reassurance, therefore, about the practicalities of certain modes of anarchism, examples given by George Woodcock will be found worthy of consideration. He tells the story of Josiah Warren, an early nineteenth century anarchist who had been influenced by Robert Owen. He made *"labour for labour"* his formula and *"sought to find means of putting into effective practice Owen's original proposal for an exchange of labour time on an hour-for-hour basis, but with a flexibility that would allow individuals to agree on some kind of adjustment when one man's work, irrespective of time, had clearly been more arduous than another's."*

When he returned from New Harmony to Cincinnati, he started his first experiment — a *"Time Store"* which he hoped would enable him to *"recruit supporters willing to take part in his plans to found a chain of mutualist villages."* His aim was to teach his customers the meaning of *"exchange based on labour"* by selling goods at cost price and asking customers to give him notes promising to donate time at their own occupations, to repay him for his trouble. After three years in the Time Store, Warren was convinced his plan was workable and *"he spent the next two years on what seems to have been the first design for a rotary press, and out of the earnings from his patents in stereotyping he accumulated enough money to start in 1833 a journal entitled "**The Peaceful Revolutionist.**"* When his ideas became known through his publications, he was able to enter on *"the final stage in his carefully planned scheme of action."*

This was to found a model village, and to this end, he and his disciples founded the Village of Equity on land purchased in Ohio in 1834. Six families *"built their houses and operated a co-operative sawmill on a labour-for-labour exchange basis."* They decided on simple mutual agreements instead of using *"the hierarchical structure of the Owenite and Fourierite Communities ... and it was in fact the first anarchist community in any country since Winstanley's venture on St George's Hill almost two centuries before."* The settlement was on low-lying land and there was malaria among the settlers and, finally, a `flu epidemic, which brought the community to an end. The exchange system *"hardly had time to prove itself."*

Warren's persistence and conviction of the *"essential practicality of his theories"* led to his founding a second colony, in 1846, called Utopia. The organisation of the colony was *"as near pure individualist anarchism as seems humanly possible"* and, for some years, the community was *"virtually independent of outside society"*, working brick kilns, stone quarries and saw-mills on the Warrenite basis.

In the Spring of 1848, Warren wrote:

> *Throughout our operations on the ground, everything has been conducted so nearly upon the individualist basis that not one meeting for legislation has taken place. No organization, no indefinite delegated power, no constitutions, no laws or bye-laws, rules or regulations but such as each individual makes for himself and his own business. No officers, no priests nor prophets have been resorted to — nothing of either kind has been in demand.*

He went on to report that their only meetings had been for social reasons: *"friendly conversation"*, music, dancing etc. It had not even been necessary to give a lecture on the principles they were acting upon for, as one lady remarked. *"The subject once stated and understood, there is nothing left to talk about"* — only action.

Utopia, with about a hundred inhabitants and some small woodworking industries, lasted for almost twenty years, in spite of Warren's departure in 1850. He then founded Modern Times, on Long Island, *"which also maintained its mutualist character for at least two decades, eventually turning, like Utopia, into a more or less conventional village with cooperative tendencies."*

Woodcock points out that *"neither community can be counted an actual failure"*, mainly because, due to the Civil War, American society was in a state of fluidity and, in fact, both communities *"tended to dissolve rather than collapse as society in the eastern United States became more stabilized ..."*

Spain

Eighty years later, there was another civil war — the Spanish — even more ghastly than the American had been. The outcome of this was the destruction of the most extensive anarchist system in history. It clearly held great promise as a movement of the people.

We are told that public services in cities and towns *"were as adequately operated as they had been before the Civil War and that some, at least of the factories were run remarkably well. Spanish communal traditions and the long absorption of anarchist teachings of voluntary cooperation seem to have borne good fruit."*

It is further noted that collectivization in the rural areas was extensive in the beginning. The French writer, Gaston Leval, is quoted as saying there were 500 collectives in the Levante, 400 in Aragon, 230 in Castile and, in Andalusia, *"every village that escaped the first onslaught of the nationalists automatically collectivised its land"* and he estimated that, by 1937, there were three million people living in collectivized local economies.

We are told about variations in standards of living and work in the different regions. In Andalusia, the goal was a simplification of living that would produce *"a dignified, free and equal poverty"*, whereas in Aragon and Catalonia there was a tendency towards *"scientific agriculture and as much mechanization as possible"* in order to improve methods of cultivation. Ambitious plans for ending adult literacy were set up in almost all the collectivized villages and attempts were made *"to create medical services and to provide for the care of the people unable to work."*

It seems that the success of agrarian collectivization was difficult to assess because the advance of the nationalist troops appears to have put a stop to it after two-and-a-half farm seasons at most, and in some areas after the first harvest, but *"the one great achievement was that, for the first time within living memory in many parts of rural Spain, there was work and food, if not luxury, for all. Land that had gone untilled for generations was cultivated again, and no man starved."* However, the government began to interfere with distribution systems, which *"were often inefficient"* and peasants growing *"specialized crops, such as oranges or olives, which had lost their normal foreign markets, probably suffered a great deal more than those who carried on mixed or grain farming and lived largely from their own produce."*

It appears that many observers are sufficiently convinced of the success of the peasants of the anarchist regions as to believe *"that collectivization of some kind is still the only real solution to the perennial problem of the land in Spain."*

I come at last to the insurrection of June, the most extensive and the most singular that has occurred in our history, and perhaps in any other: the most extensive, because, during four days, more than a hundred thousand men were engaged in it; the most singular, because the insurgents fought without a war-cry, without leaders, without flags, and yet with a marvellous harmony and an amount of military experience that astonished the oldest officers. (de Tocqueville, walking through Paris during the revolution of 1848).

Chapter Nine

The Microcosm: Leaderless Groups

Self-managing groups are faced with problems of decision-making, from the first instant of assuming collective responsibility. Simple but basic matters, such as times and frequency of meeting, venue and seating arrangements, all established by regular usage, will be proposed for review, or change. There are always some alternatives, so a decision must be reached which, in turn, requires a review of how a decision is to be reached. Discussions certainly, but then — by apparent consensus? By a majority vote? By a unanimous assent, person by person? And after such a decision has been achieved, there will be other issues which, again, turn out not to be as simple as they appear.

Is there to be an agenda for the next meeting? For every meeting? Is a priority list of concerns to be drawn up? If so, how, and by whom? Are decisions, or discussion, somehow to be recorded? For what purpose and by whom?

Then, most difficult usually, if a decision is reached, how is it to be implemented? Will responsibility be accepted by one of the members? Can it be imposed on one or more, or can it be shared among the group? If shared, is it agreed, is it even clear, who will accept responsibility for what, exactly? And then, what about resources? Time will probably be the first scarce resource, followed perhaps by competence. Who is seen as likely to have sufficient time to undertake the task in hand? And is that person seen as the most competent? Can manual or secretarial assistance be allocated? Will money be involved? Can the group command it? Is the distribution of such resources agreed? All of which is no more than the beginning. The group may find at a subsequent meeting that nothing has been done. What sanctions then are available to constrain the action required?

A group may meet regularly, perhaps for months, in a determined effort to reach finality on such issues, only to find agreement still eludes them. The resolution of an issue opens out into a series of other issues. Furthermore, an issue decided does not always stay decided. It is common to find that a decision is taken that a particular topic shall be the main item for consideration at the next meeting; and, in the event, no one seems interested in discussing it. If there were a chairperson, he/she would be expected to drive the group through the necessary stages to deal with the topic, but the whole purpose of the leaderless group is to experience what happens when there is no driver. If a group makes for itself a series of decisions on time, place, the conduct of meetings, the registration of further decisions, methods of implementation and allocation of responsibility for action, then that constitutes a body of common laws, sometimes a written code, perhaps an administrative apparatus and an executive arm. What happens, then, when individuals do not obey the laws, or do not perform their duties? This is a matter of discipline. At the societal level, there are police, who have the special function of enforcing compliance with the law. In a small group, the whole membership may, explicitly or not, take on the function of a court to try the delinquent and pronounce sentence. But who is to enforce their decision?

What is to happen if an entire group fails to carry through its own decisions? This is, in fact, quite a common situation. It may seem as if the group had, at one stage, decided *"What we really ought to do is ..."* *"It would be very nice if everybody ..."* This exposes law as a set of aspirations rather than an encoding of real intentions. Currently, there is a very necessary concern for human rights, extending to all countries. It becomes obvious that repressive regimes, known to be guilty of the most hideous abuses, have embodied prescriptions guaranteeing the rights and freedom of the citizen into their own legal codes. They proclaim the fact, whenever accused of abuses.

It becomes clear that societal functions are mirrored in small group functions. The problems of self-management in the group are laid open for examination, and are seen to illuminate those of the firm, or the nation. These include the processes of decision-making, the structure for supporting these processes, administrative systems and executive arms, the codification of law and its enforcement. There are others relating to the expression of opinion, the seeking out of undeclared opinion, the modality of discussion or debate, assumptions of status and the distribution of privilege, the misuse of majority power to crush minorities. The self-conscious and often painfully slow process of small-group analysis will expose all such issues. It is thus a most important means of learning and of consciousness-raising. The tendency has been to see the value of small-group experiences as related to self-knowledge, personal growth, professional skills and *"sensitivity training"*. It is, of course, the royal road towards all of those ends. For immediate purposes, the stress has been placed on the universal exigencies of the group as a group, and as revealing so much that we need to understand about structures and processes in the social system overall.

If the analogy (but it is more than an analogy) between group processes and societal process is followed through, some suggestive observations present themselves. At both levels, there will be a wish for a strong and competent leader. In a small group, the possibility and the satisfaction of transcending that wish may be experienced. The discomforts of uncertainty may be followed by rejection of leadership and then, at a more mature phase, the re-absorption of the former non-leader into the group structure as a valued specialist — at the service of the group, rather than in command of it. One may then speculate whether something may be learned from experiencing such transition of relevance for the understanding of any historical revolt of the masses, where a king or dictator has been executed; or of a local event, where an established union leader has been displaced in favour of a group of representatives.

The Psychology of Groups

Group psychology is a twentieth century development which rapidly established itself as significant for theory and for practice. From its roots in the 1920s; its applications in industry and in World War II, it took new forms during the 1950s and 1960s, then burgeoned in such variety that it has become almost impossible to take account of its seemingly endless proliferation. Much of this is dramatic and ephemeral; for our present purpose, we shall look back to the 1930s and 1940s, when the fundamentals of group dynamics were first clearly revealed.

We may note first the well-known work on mule spinning, assembly, wiring and other tasks, by Elton Mayo in the General Electric Company in the United States. This demonstrated unequivocally that the behaviour of line workers could not be sufficiently accounted for in terms of individual response to changing material conditions, but that a collective factor was in evidence. Their relations with authority figures appeared to be significant, and the recognition of their possible motivation and existence as persons was reflected in productivity, and in a shared positive attitude. To this observation, the term morale was applied, which had long been established in military usage. It had always been obvious in war that the collective willingness of troops to maintain discipline, to continue to fight when in great danger, in many instances even to the point of annihilation, was a variable phenomenon. The collective will could suddenly disappear, replaced by a concern for the individual self. In group settings, this came to be known as fight/flight. Leadership was recognised as the key factor, but the early attempts to understand it and to identify the characteristics of effective leadership were soon shown to be quite inadequate. It remained to be explained, for instance, why *"bad"* leaders could, apparently secure the loyal devotion of whole nations, or why a quiet person, by-passed in the search for what had mistakenly been seen as leadership qualities, could, on occasion, be successful when given responsibility for a group.

A new approach to the understanding of leadership was provided by Freud in 1922, with his publication of **Group Psychology and the Analysis of the Ego**. As with all his contributions, this work broke new ground: it did not provide conclusive resolutions of the problems involved, but it set in train certain modes of thought, and later of practice, in the fields of group psychology, collective behaviour and social psychology generally. In part, Freud's focus was on the projection of archaic aspects of the personality onto dangerous or hero figures.

In the application of psycho-analytic insights to group therapy, the pioneering work of Foulkes has not received due recognition. From the late 1930s, somewhat in advance of developments in the Tavistock Clinic, he carefully deployed the Freudian skills of listening and tentative interpretation of the phenomena of the individual in the group and of the group itself.

In his account of the early development of group therapy, J.B. Nichol summarises Foulkes' findings that, whilst the group retains the fundamental agents of individual therapy — in catharsis, transference, (to a limited extent) and the bringing into consciousness of repressed material — important additional factors are involved. Individuals can identify with others or react against them; the projection process becomes *"transparent"* and this leads to important insight into the self and relations outside the group; they develop a continuing relationship with the other group members, feeling able to show their understanding of others, as well as feeling that others understand them. Anxiety and guilt are relieved when they realise that other people have similar morbid experiences, and an important spin-off of this is that *"other people's suffering puts their own into perspective."* Nichol highlights what Foulkes referred to as the mirror reaction — the fact that it is easier to recognise other people's problems and consider ways in which they might be resolved, which in turn leads the patient to identify with others and analyse his own reactions. Arising out of all this, there is *"a particular tone in the quality of the relationship"* with the others, which Foulkes called resonance. These important concepts, which Foulkes introduced, are phenomena peculiar to the group situation.

Freud believed that in the group situation, an individual's judgement and freedom of thought were limited by a mysterious bond — he used hypnotism and suggestion as analogies. His conclusion was that a repressed attachment to the leader (often expressed as its opposite) was the ultimate emotional factor; that group members share in this extension of an original family situation, which enables them to unite and identify with each other.

Freud's early colleague and biographer, Ernest Jones, wrote:

> ... *the parallels he drew between group and individual motivation were more than analogies. They point to a profound genetic connection, and in consequence it has become increasingly hard for sociologists to pursue their investigations of institutions on a social basis alone. If, for instance, we are ever to come nearer to the apparently insoluble problem of the most suitable form of Government it can only be through taking seriously into account the comparison between the relations of governed to governors and that of children to parents, and also those between children themselves. The necessity for power and force in restrained measure and on the other hand the almost invariable abuse of such power provide problems the solution of which would benefit the world enormously.*

This exactly expresses the issue with which this text is also concerned. These considerations are relevant for our concern with group processes. The view of behaviour as generated within the family gives rise to the hope that it may be socially modified, and that groups in which social processes are most intense and most exposed could be the primary instrument for achieving this. This expectation has met with a limited success. Psycho-drama, in which people re-enact past traumas; socio-drama, in which roles may be taken and exchanged; encounter groups, in which members reflect truthfully how they perceive and react to other members; transactional analysis, in which members may become aware of their own compulsions and life-scripts — all of these have great potential for extending and deepening self-awareness. Their potential for helping people to resolve the ensuing conflicts is much less certain.

The Tavistock Institute

The leaderless group, however, at least as developed within the Tavistock Institute, has been concerned with the behaviour of the group as a group, rather than with the personalities of individual members. As the thinking was derived from Freud, so the method can be considered an adaptation of the Freudian psychoanalysis, in that the analyst chose to remain silent, except for occasional brief and gnomic contributions. This had the inevitable effect of leaving the group in a state of confusion. It was clear that they expected a lead from the analyst. As he refused to supply it, they would seek to repair the deficiency from their own resources.

Individuals would be put forward, or would more or less explicitly offer themselves. Such initiatives, without formal establishment, proved to be unsatisfactory to the group, and of brief duration. Proposals might be made for some variety of formal procedure, perhaps to include voting for a member or for a topic; the group was *"seeking a structure"*, but none emerged. Members would feel they had, to some extent, been deceived, as they had expected that the analyst named as in some way responsible would somehow take the group. Experience has shown, however, that even when the principles of the method, and even the processes likely to emerge, are described in the advance literature, people arrive with expectations of something else. This is not surprising, because what happens in the event is outside the range of their normal experience. The paradox is that what they are invited to recognise in their own behaviour and that of others is very familiar. It is a matter of recognising what happens every day under their own noses.

It will be seen that the method derives directly from Freudian innovation of the 1890s. When Freud repudiated doctor's orders, refused to direct or even advise his neurotic patients but, instead, only to listen to them without interruption for hundreds of hours, he broke with aeons of medical presumption. The change was revolutionary: there were profound democratic implications, which have never been fully explicated. He was the great revolutionary, but one who never disclaimed his own authority. There have been other examples of this phenomenon, notably, that of Karl Marx.

Freud's method, ostensibly developed for therapeutic purposes, which, to some extent, it was able to accomplish, was most fruitful in the generation of new knowledge and significant hypotheses — although Freud was not much interested in the experimental hypothetical-inductive approach to mental science. While not identifying generalisation with idiocy, as did Blake, he may be said to have followed Blake, in that his own strength lay in the exhaustive examination of the *"minute particulars"*. His endless patience in listening sprang from an equally insatiable wish to know, ultimately a curiosity with infantile roots. He might well have said, *"We know virtually nothing about the unceasing torrent of our mental life. We need a method that will do some justice to its complexity, even if it requires years of attention to the self-disclosures of one person."* This was utterly original.

It was a natural step for the Freudian-trained analysts of the Tavistock Institute to apply the method in their work with groups. They, too had therapeutic intentions, but generated interpretative concepts that were mainly fruitful for research. As with the work of Freud, himself, these were not formulated as testable hypotheses, but by a process of diffusion came to inform the thinking of group workers in the training, remedial, therapeutic and community fields, most of whom would not be especially concerned to trace the historical origins of their own understanding.

The most influential articles that emerged from practice with groups were those of W.R. Bion from 1948-1952, and in book form as **Experiences in Groups**. It is not easy to read or understand, though it has an ironic humour.

Many of the principal concepts are not so difficult. They have become part of the common currency of group work, as it was possible to observe the patterns of behaviour from which they were derived in groups of every kind. Bion called them basic assumptions, shared by a group which were as follows:

Dependence, in which a group appears to be happy with their leader and with his proposals, but proves to have little commitment to the task of carrying them through. Then there is fight/flight, in which suggestions for action are aggressively rejected, or avoided by discussing trivial aspects of them. Pairing has reference to the situation where group members become involved with other members on an individual basis, apparently deriving some private satisfaction from this engagement, at the cost of contributing to the group task. Counterposed to these avoidance mechanisms, there is the Work group, which has accepted its task and makes progress with it. Work groups, in which members share an orientation towards accomplishing their task, can be astonishingly productive. The switch from a state of disharmony and discomfort may be sudden. A physicist member of such a group characterised the change as *"flip-flop steady-state"* — and so it may appear.

A secondary but significant manifestation recognised by most participants early in the life of a group is the toleration of silences. This is associated with a recognition that most people are uncomfortable in silences, perhaps even feeling that one's own silence is impolite to others. It is discovered that much small talk serves the purpose of excluding silences, in which unpleasant feelings may surface from within the self. This has the good effect of bringing about the replacement of polite empty talk by a shared assumption that one is only to speak when one has something genuine to express. So the content of the exchanges in the group is deepened.

This is the point at which the group accepts some responsibility for itself, at the same time renouncing its earlier expectations of the appointed leader, though he may come to be seen as occupying a different role as consultant expert.

It appeared as if group analysts, who soon had a reputation for saying nothing, or hardly anything (and that barely intelligible) in the groups they took, were also saying *"We know virtually nothing about the unceasing torrent of mental life in groups. We also need to listen in silence to the disclosures and manifestations of group life, because we find there most of the basic constituents of all social interaction and of society itself."*

So the group came to be seem as a microcosm of the greater society. Observations could be made, as Kurt Lewin had already done, of groups under democratic or authoritarian leadership, or the apparent near-anarchy resulting from the laissez faire principle. But it seemed more promising to observe totally free-running groups, with no appointed leader and no imposed constraints, so that the protean changes and sudden transformations could manifest themselves with a minimum of extraneous influence.

The experiential mini-society, pioneered by Gunnar Hjelholt in 1967, is worthy of note. This has to be a group event of sufficient size and duration to permit differentiation of status and resources to be brought into play, and for social developments to run their consequential course. Miller and Brown (1985) have described events succeeding each other in bewildering variety during a 3-day Mini-Economy they set up in 1984, attempting *"to explore the way in which interpersonal behaviour is affected by economic structures."* A currency was created, and a sharply graded system of allowances, valid for bedroom accommodation, meals and drinks (which some could not afford). The organisers constituted themselves as civil servants. There were 34 participants. *"Civil Service inundated with job applications ... Kitchen and dining room taken over by a group demanding redistribution of wealth ... free breakfasts ... full support of the Assembly ... wealthy group buys franchise to all bedrooms ... civil service opens bank; raided, accounts stolen ... civil service resign ... refused food ... Assembly buys franchise ... bedrooms free — all now Comrades... kitchen staff appoint themselves Lords of the Kitchen ... refuse food to non-workers ... civil service appointed King and Queen."* A participant writes: *"During the first 24 hours we managed to condense five centuries of social change; we lived through capitalism, revolution, socialism and feudalism."*

Unscripted play-acting will usually generate significant phenomena. Moreno's successful use of psycho-drama (1930+) was the earliest exploitation of it as a method. The rapidly succeeding dramas of the mini-society reflect and illuminate some of the structures and processes in which the participants are involved in real life. We also need to note the swiftly changing leadership and decision processes in a society without formally appointed leaders.

We might remember that the enlightenment of the 18th century, which provided for freedom from arbitrary power, a right to freedom of information and the expression of one's own opinion, to a separation of the judiciary from the legislative authority, to the equality of citizens before the law, to trial before an independent jury and, ultimately, to a voice in the selection of one's rulers — all of this might never have happened, so far as the average industrial firm is concerned. The factory worker knows that freedom of speech is limited to conversation with his fellow workers. He knows that the consequences could be drastic if he voiced his opinion to supervisors, middle or top management, of their conduct of affairs. He also knows that he can safely express all his views to his local elective counsellors, and often enough to salaried officials if he has access to them. Why the discrepancy? In private industry, only the owners, the shareholders, have the powers of the final decision. This is increasingly recognised as unjust, especially where long-term employees, whose livelihoods are at stake, are excluded. *"Stakeholders"* is the term now used, and their rights are coming to be discussed as a matter of equity. In producer co-operatives, the power system is turned upside down. They, at least, have attained to the understanding of the 18th century.

T-Groups offer a field of observation of unparalleled richness. Virtually all that is looked for, and found in the T-Groups may be observed in the large collective. Interpretations may be valid across the range. The wish for a leader and for a structure are particularly impressive; universal, perhaps. Open conflict is valued, as a necessary revelation of reality. This may be seen as the key principle in direct democracy.

Chapter Ten

Possibilities and Resistances

In the spirit of Nietzsche's declaration that a well-rounded theory is an act of bad faith, little attempt will be made to gather together all the threads of argument that have been started in this text into a coherent ending. For one thing, the forms of participative democracy are infinitely various. For another, many of the fields of possible implementation are familiar to us all: the reader will wish to reach his own conclusion in each case, indeed will insist on doing so. There is certainly a central theme which runs throughout, and calls for re-emphasis at the point of signing off: this is the indissoluble connection between collective self-government, adult learning and the quality of life. What follows, however, is more concerned with issues not discussed in the foregoing chapters.

Cultural Variables

Some cultures have a propensity towards general participation, some against it. It is said that the ancient Greeks were disposed towards it because they had always been accustomed to continuous talk, bargaining and argument in the agora and afterwards — with traders from other lands. The Roman forum later became rather more of an elite preserve for the practice of rhetoric. Some tribal cultures, which manifest open general argumentation on policy, already exemplify the essential principle. Other tribal systems may be essentially authoritarian. Moslem cultures, and others which segregate women, however much they may be valued, will have difficulties with open participation. Co-operation in Sweden, based on the Rochdale 1844 model, has been far more successful than the original. Probably because the culture was less biassed against workers and against women, who are predominant in consumption, the co-operative store could become a leader in design, respected by all classes. Would Robert Owen's New Lanark experiment have been more successful if he had set it up among his own people, the Welsh? Would co-operatives have been less successful if the innovation had been made in Yorkshire, where men "manned" the woollen mills, rather than in Lancashire, where cotton spinning and weaving were women's work in the main? Why was it that in some Swiss cantons, work in the small factories was thought appropriate only for women, while the men managed the farms; and in other cantons these roles were reversed? And how have these differences been reflected in their small-scale local democracies?

All of this suggests that if we are persuaded of the validity of the participative principle, we are to expect that responses to any initiative proposed will vary, sometimes sharply, in accord with local cultures.

The Swiss Case

Direct democracy, in its various possible forms of collective decision-making, is commonly thought of as (a) wildly impractical, and (b) a far-out radical nostrum to enshrine left-wing factions permanently in the seats of power. Both of these assumptions are disproved by the experience of Switzerland over more than a century. The routes whereby the will of the peoples of the 26 cantons is brought into effect at the level of federal government are open for all to see and to operate. Certain limitations, delays and constraints have been built into the system, and are accepted; but the local assemblies, the initiatives and the referenda are all in evidence, and are incorporated in the processes of government, year by year. They function in parallel and with interaction with the more familiar representative institutions, one of which is composed of elected part-time members who have other vocations, and meet in session four times a year, for three week periods only. The advantages of a parliament whose members are not professional politicians has often been debated.

Some of the cantons were small, and a few of them still are. They are living examples of decision-making by a public meeting, sometimes of thousands of citizens. Swiss accounts of the operation of their system elude the argument of this book, in that it seems to be assumed that in the larger cantons, and in the federal system, a representative system, based on voting, becomes necessary.

The practicality of the Swiss system, forged over generations, is not in question: it is there for all to see. Of more interest for some will be its conservative tendency. For those with experience of genuinely free discussion, this will be no surprise. Teachers experimenting with such methods, as a form of social education among older school pupils, have often been perplexed to find that the young people (though not in all schools) would like to stop immigration from Asian countries, would favour the re-introduction of capital and corporal punishment, and are ambivalent about equal status for women. The Swiss men debated in their assemblies for something like a hundred years whether women should participate and should have the vote. It was not until 1971 that political equality for women was made a formal requirement at federal level. We might consider how long the United States would have taken to achieve the abolition of slavery, if the decision had rested with thousands of local assemblies.

Radicals have seen total participation in decision-making as the golden road to empowerment of the people; as virtually identical with it, in fact. It can be disappointing to observe that when such empowerment is achieved — which is very rare — collectives prove to be self-interested. It is predictable that in the green suburbia around an industrial city, one will find a well-off, well-connected and articulate body of citizens, able to fend off the planners' proposals to situate an open prison, a unit for sub-normal adults, or even a Sikh temple, in their open spaces. If the less privileged over-spill housing estate residents say: *"Why should we have it all: new factories and urban motorways as well?"*, their protests are likely to be less effective.

What is at stake here is not a matter of cognitive understanding. Rather, it is the entire formation of persons in their historical relations, and the prevailing ethos, that is at issue.

The Swiss have done well for themselves in recent decades, in allowing their own interests to over-ride those of the high proportion of Yugoslav, Turkish and Italian guest-workers, on whom their prosperity has so largely depended: and one looks through their official publications in vain for any recognition of the vast wealth accrued by their acceptance of the deposited funds of the world's great kleptocrats, the drug-derived wealth of the great Latin American operators; and the Mafia itself. The strictly maintained confidentiality of their great banking systems may be seen as a collectively endorsed international conspiracy.

The Menace of Bureaucracy

In their paper **"Inquiry into Participation — a research approach"**, United States Research Institute for Social Development, Andrew Pearse and Matthias Stiefel state that many present-day democratic countries have introduced *"democracy by delegation"* — even those where a system of direct democracy formerly functioned. By this, they mean that a small group is elected *"to represent the view of the broader electorate"*, on the assumption that *"there is parallelism between the opinions and wishes of the masses with* *those expressed or pursued by their chosen representatives."*

There is, however, an increasing feeling among popular groups (even in the industrialised western world) that their participation in the political decision-making processes is minimal, and this has led to the formation of action groups. This, in turn has led governments to decide that political stability is under threat, as well as the prevailing distribution of power and wealth. Pearse and Stiefel go on to say:

> *In societies where some formal elements of participation exist, the level actually permitted may be tacitly determined by class position or ethnic character; or perhaps the majority of the population may be granted token participation that serves the purposes of control rather than the sharing of responsibility and power; or they may be societies in which customary institutionalized participation won in past struggles has turned obsolete and ineffective and has been outflanked by new forms of manipulation and control, by discriminatory ideologies, or by the use of mass media, or by the hardening of bureaucratic arteries.*

Where a participatory movement is led by a single individual, on the basis of either traditional social status, democratic election or personal charisma, the fate of the movement is often linked to his personal fate and, whilst collective leadership seems to ensure greater continuity, it *"seems more difficult to achieve."*

Pearse and Stiefel then begin to identify the anti-participatory structures:

> *... it must be accepted, therefore, that the struggle for people's participation implies an attempted redistribution of both control of resources and of power in favour of those who live by their own productive labour. This situation has very difficult implications which must be faced squarely. Under what circumstances and to what extent will governments establish or tolerate participatory institutions and organizations which "empower" the worker, the citizen, the share tenant, the field-labourer, the tribal, the petty cultivator, the artisan and the fisherman? How far will they wish to promote or control such movements? How will they react to participatory movements that seek improved livelihood outside the framework of official institutions?* (p.5).

> *Bureaucracies, complex technologies and industrial enterprises all tend to be anti-participatory by nature, and to impose conditions that make little provision for popular participation, yet their failure to serve humane values and to improve the quality of life seems due to this very*

lack of participation by those directly affected. For this reason, there seems to be more hope for participation arising from uncontainable pressure from below than from the programmes imposed by the bureaucracies from above. (p.26).

In *The New Internationalist* (12/86), Martin Stott reports that the co-operative approach *"has little use for the static, wasteful and bureaucratic structures of state ownership."* His alternative could be a pluralistic public sector that is accountable to local communities through municipal initiatives and regional or sector-based enterprise boards — whose aims are broader than maximising profit. They would recognise the need for social criteria that take account of what is produced (*socially useful production*), how it is produced (*human-centred technology*), for whom — and with what external effects, eg. environmental.

This is excellent. However, it invites some questions. First, the proposed system of accountability is highly complex. Co-operatives may group themselves under municipalities; or regional boards; or sectoral boards. Presumably, there would need to be a system of co-ordination between these, to obviate the too familiar private enterprise phenomena of sudden-death closures, and to bring transport, housing, road systems and all public services into relation with the co-operatives, private enterprises, and each other; some kind of planning, in fact. Would it be possible to achieve that without some kind of bureaucracy not too dissimilar from that which already exists? Second, if co-operatives are to be locally accountable, which is most desirable as a general principle, there remains the problem of the accountability of the local authorities themselves. To their own citizens, undoubtedly; to national government and its administrative arms, inevitably; to regional planning and co-ordinating boards, as far as possible; and to a number of over-arching sectoral bodies concerned with agriculture, transport, power, police, water etc., in considerable variety. Could this be achieved without bureaucracy? At what level in a hierarchy can the co-operative principle continue to be valid?

There can be no general answer to this question. It will vary in relation to the function of a system, the structure it has developed to accomplish its purposes, its general usages and understandings that enable its members to act in accordance with expectations. It was once said that Unilever operates through a hundred and fifty companies which have autonomy in respect of their special products. This is contrasted with Shell, an even larger transnational corporation, which has one main product and can, therefore, operate very much as a single coherent organism. Constituent companies of

Unilever, or some of them, at least, could conceivably be bought out by their workers, and continue to have a special relation with the parent company. The Shell structure would not seem open to such a possibility. This example is enough to give pause to any intention to work out general monitoring of co-operative enterprise by a Department of Trade and Industry, or whatever may replace it. An understanding of the mode of operation of co-operatives, together with a commitment to their values and principles, are the essentials.

A large proportion of the Peruvian economy is informal; it consists of very small enterprises that escape bureaucratic regulation. It may take a year to register a dress-maker, four years for a bus company. The fact that so many Peruvians are able to survive in circumstances that to most of us would seem utterly hopeless, would not surprise anarchists who might think the population could look after itself better if the government did not attempt to help. But it must be said that conditions in some areas where a government has not been able to impose itself do not offer much encouragement.

There are bureaucratic systems of such complexity that a high proportion of the energy of highly paid officials is absorbed in relations with each other. Moreover, such systems are wicked enough to defend themselves. They strive officiously to keep alive. In the last days of the Soviet Union, permission was given to farms to buy pedigree stock from the West, to raise investment funds and to sell to Britain or France; but the regulations also decreed that all was to be *"in keeping with established procedure"*, and *"in combination with state guidance."* That is all a bureaucrat needs.

Michael Rustin, however, cautions us against an unconsidered rejection of bureaucracy and bureaucrats in these terms:

> *We unjustly abuse public services and those whose work it is to provide them by too readily endorsing the criticisms of their enemies. Whilst we need to remember that service-providers can confuse their own interests with those of their clients, we have also to defend traditions of public service as an indispensable resource. If we accept that disinterested practices of public service are next to impossible, we might as well abandon any idea of socialism.* (New Left Review 175, June, 1989.)

That responsible participation in collective decision-making necessarily induces essential social learning in depth is obvious enough. If it does not receive public recognition in our time, this must surely be because those in control of our affairs across the whole spectrum — in industry, in administration, in education, social work or medicine — fear it. With no knowledge of participation, they fear to lose control, while still being held accountable. They lack experience of the support and facilitation a collective offers to a trusted leader.

A Marxist Critique

Ernest Mandel has been perhaps the most widely read Marxian economist of our generation. He has identified what he considers to be the fatal weakness of self-management as a basis for socialist government. His analysis is representative of much Marxist criticism of the claims made for co-operation. He sees socialism as essentially class-based, co-operatives as group-based. These are seen as incompatible. Groups will necessarily compete with each other. The more loyalty groups attract, the less will be available for a socialist party representing the interests of workers as a whole. Some co-operatives will be more successful than others, and will strive to improve their position even further. At any given starting point, some groups will be more favoured than others in terms of plant, managerial skill, access to resources or to markets. Equal effort, equal devotion to the tasks of production will lead to an increasing disparity of incomes. Locked into fierce competition between themselves, workers will never form a coherent party, strong enough to challenge and overthrow the bastions of national and international capital and their political agents.

> *It is, thus, to deceive the workers to lead them to believe that they can manage their affairs at the level of the factory. In the present economic system, a whole series of decisions are inevitably taken at higher levels than the factory, and if these decisions are not consciously made by the working class as a whole, then they will be made by other forces in society behind the workers' backs.* Cited by Ken Coates in *The New Worker Co-operatives*, **Spokesman Pamphlet.**

Mandel points out that Yugoslavia, whose economy functioned on a basis of co-operative units, never resolved this problem:

> *They are faced with an unenviable decision. On the one hand, they can accept the logic of rationalisations: reduction of the labour force, speed-up, and so on. On the other, they can reject this logic, thus condemning certain units of production to operate at a loss and to pay wages far below average rates.*

One might perhaps reply to Mandel that the long-standing discontents of the ethnic Albanians in Kosovo are not entirely of this character. No doubt *"wages far below average rates"* were a factor. But Mandel's solution, stated without hesitation or qualification, is somewhat bland, to say the least:

> *The only solution to all these questions is to regulate industry at a social level thus allowing for an effectively planned economy consciously run by the working class as a whole, and for the process of depolarisation to advance.*

After all, Yugoslavia made honest attempts to achieve that. It did not leave the prosperous Slovenes feeling any happier. They knew very well that they could do even better for themselves if they were allowed to break free and manage their own finances. They may have seen the justice of the claims of Macedonia for social help and capital investment, and not felt that such claims should have priority over their own urgent needs for more motorways to accommodate their burgeoning traffic.

The problems of reconciling the competing claims of groups and minorities in great variety, with each other and with overriding national imperatives, do not yield to any ideological prescriptions. One expects to find the greatest resistance amongst the oppressed and impoverished, but recent history suggests that it is the rich, or potentially rich, peoples who are setting problems for their governments.

The possibility of international warfare remains as a threat, rather than an actuality. Since world war II, the focus has shifted, and continues to shift, towards internal struggles, which have become the main field of action of national armies. They are called upon to suppress armed revolt, everything labelled as "terrorism", and to defend the formal integrity of a nation. From Katanga and Biafra, the Kurds, Cypriot Turks and others too numerous to list, until our day, we see Timor, the Tamils, the Basques, the Sikhs — again, the list is almost endless — all *"rightly struggling to be free"*, by one means or another. Latin America, Central Africa (eg. the Tutsi) even Australia, provide examples of near genocide. The South African government bloodily suppressed its black peoples, suppressed information and news access and, ultimately, suppressed even its suppression of information.

In the United Kingdom, the Scots are becoming more aware of the indifference and exploitation they experience at the hands of the English London-based government. The point in rehearsing this familiar catalogue is to stress that the conflicts of minority interests within nations are perennial. There is no prospect that they can be eliminated, because nations themselves are historical artifacts — imposed on territories to which other people may have a claim. They like to present an ancient image of themselves that subjects may accept as an identity and be willing to die for. Such claims are usually factitious, transparently so in many instances. Most of the world's nations are of recent foundation and their existence is precarious. They exist largely to serve the purposes of a privileged elite, and they are open to challenge from within, with just cause. Their status is always open to question.

The phenomena of ethnic identity, clearly a major dynamic on the world scene, have never been acceptably theorised. This is an area where Marxism has failed. There is more promise in the psychoanalytic approach to group phenomena, recognising parent figures, projection, dependency, the Kleinian *"paranoid position"*, *"projective identification"*, good and bad *"internal objects"*. All such phenomena are visible across the range from small groups of local activists to nation states.

Mandel is right to warn of the difficulties and contradictions in the regulations of a co-operative state. He is not right to dismiss national co-operative aspirations on that account: this for two main reasons. First, these problems have never been satisfactorily resolved, under any system. Socialist states, East and West, have responded to them simply by repression. This cannot be what Mandel would wish. Second, the culture of co-operation, based on day-by-day experience of working through conflicts of interest within the group, is more propitious for the resolution of higher level issues. It may be contrasted with the fundamentalist culture — Islamic, Christian or Thatcherite — which is incapable of any accommodation. But fundamentalism, as some moderate Muslims have said, must fail, because it is against reason and against the course of history; whereas self-management shows itself to be the necessary progressive phase, when the people of the world can get free from imposed authoritarianism and the violence inseparable from it.

Social Responsibility

The question is often asked whether co-operatives contending for a place, a share of the action, in a fiercely competitive climate where mere survival is an achievement, can at the same time preserve their virtue. The answer is generally an affirmative one, if the very numerous accounts of successful small co-operatives are taken as evidence. No doubt, these are written-up by literate and aware people, often those who were involved in establishing the enterprise in the first instance. In that, they acted on principle and would not have wished to continue with their own involvement, if they had felt that some wrong turn towards irresponsible practices had been taken.

It does not seem to be the case that ethical practice necessarily entails material sacrifice. When the move towards ethical investment started in Britain, in the early 1980s (it was already active in the U.S.A.) the Friends Provident set up the Stewardship Unit Trust. Financial advisers were not inclined to recommend it to investors. They did not expect any Trust that excluded much lucrative fields as tobacco, armaments, spirits and gambling to do well. Over the first year, however, it had out-performed the index. Over five years, the score is roughly equal — it will vary with the chosen base.

Introducing his I.C.O.M. booklet, Andrew Bibby has written about

> an era where, if we dig a little deeper, we can uncover more general philosophical questions; in particular, the relationship between the autonomy of a co-operative or group and the desirability for it to be accountable in some form to wider society.

As reported earlier, Scott Bader has done well since becoming a co-operative commonwealth in 1951. The preamble to its constitution includes the following:

> G. We are agreed that in the event of a down-turn in trade we will share all remaining work rather than expect any of our members to be deprived of employment, even if this requires a reduction in earnings by all. K. We are agreed that (in addition to such disinterested services that we offer as individuals) our social responsibility extends to:
>
> 1. Limiting the products of our labour to those beneficial to the community, in particular excluding any products for the specific purpose of manufacturing weapons of war.
>
> 2. Reducing any harmful effect of our work on the natural environment by rigorously avoiding the negligent discharge of pollutants.
>
> 3. Questioning constantly whether any of our activities are unnecessarily wasteful of the earth's natural resources.

Such a practice, if faithfully observed, must generate a strong fellow-feeling amongst workers, a sense of purpose and collective responsibility. That co-operative practice does have such an effect is shown in the findings of the three-country research of the European Community team, cited in the earlier chapter. Their evidence was as firmly based as anyone could demand.

That research was quickly followed by another three-country study, headed by Frank Heller of the Tavistock Institute, and colleagues from the

Netherlands and Yugoslavia (**Decisions in Organisations**, Sage, 1988). From a mass of significant findings, two are emphasised, both relevant for the present discussion:

- the under-utilization of employees' skills and competence, which is widespread, emerges as a very significant outcome of excessively centralised power;

- contrary to previous research, conflicts are shown to play a useful role in decision-making and to be to some extent a natural consequence of employee involvement.

The value of conflict is basic for practitioners of group dynamics. It is well understood by most Quakers, and needs to be accepted by all members of co-operatives.

The under-utilization of the potential of employees is the starting point in the formation of co-operatives. At first an assumption or a point of faith, it manifests itself as a dynamic factor more powerful than had been envisaged. In co-operative practice it presents itself in two modes. The first is seen where members with knowledge, skills, experience and ideas, none of which have previously been brought into play, are now matched with a real task, and respond impressively. The second appears as incompetence, lack of knowledge and an incapacity to respond to the challenge of participation. The first is reflected in the quality of work, the quality of work experience and in the quality of life. The second calls for an adult learning system.

Already in the eighteenth century, and even earlier, the stultifying effects of mindless repetitive work had been recognised. Adam Smith, the great progenitor and apologist for the division of labour, was genuinely concerned about it. There is little need to rehearse the accounts of degradation in fields, factories, mines, ships and in the servant halls of the great houses over two centuries. Technology and electric power relieved or replaced most of the drudgery during the twentieth century, or exported it to poorer countries at subsistence wages. The degradation of mindless work has been powerfully described in every generation. To this degradation, the co-operative system offers more than an alternative: rather a positive transformation. When fully implemented, no worker can avoid experience of participation, the essential element in personal and social development.

Feminism: a Network

Feminism has a thousand points of attack, dispersed throughout the social system, geographically, hierarchically, in employment, in the family, in community life, in sport, in the churches, and most pervasively in the subtleties of gender, culture and ideology. When targets are identified, groups may be formed for an assault on the bastions of resistance, whatever form they may take. There is no overall command structure. Protest takes local, spontaneous and non-hierarchical forms. They share, or tend to, a perception of existing forms of social organisation as emanating from a patriarchal, male-dominated or male- oriented view of the world. This common perception gives rise to some degree of mutuality. It is the essential basis for generation of a network.

A network, at least in its ideal form, has no hierarchy, and no centre. There may be a register of membership, and there may be a secretary, a function rotating among members. The principle is that anyone may initiate anything and inform others. If the initiative is widely felt to be appropriate, it will gather strength and support. If it is felt to be out of line, then it will wither.

The prime instance of such a network has been the anti-nuclear protest at Greenham Common, which endured for years. It took the form of a makeshift camp, irregularly spaced around the miles of perimeter fence enclosing the American nuclear base. In carrying out their orders to evict the women, the police were baffled because no leader, no chief woman, no responsible person could be found. To be completely effective, it would have been necessary to station small squads of police at intervals of a few yards. They could not knock out the organisation, because there was none.

The examples of Che Guevara and Ho Chi Min, showed that guerillas could defeat immense military machines because they themselves had no similar organisation. Certainly they received every kind of expert advice and support, but a community-based guerilla network, often with the traditional skills of the peasantry, seems able to re-constitute itself after any local attack.

The diagram opposite illustrates a network developed from the Hattersley Community Centre by Dr Margaret Ledwith during the 1980s. It could not show the inter-linkage that will have developed as needed between the one hundred entities located on it. An organic analogy is called for: the autonomic nervous system perhaps.

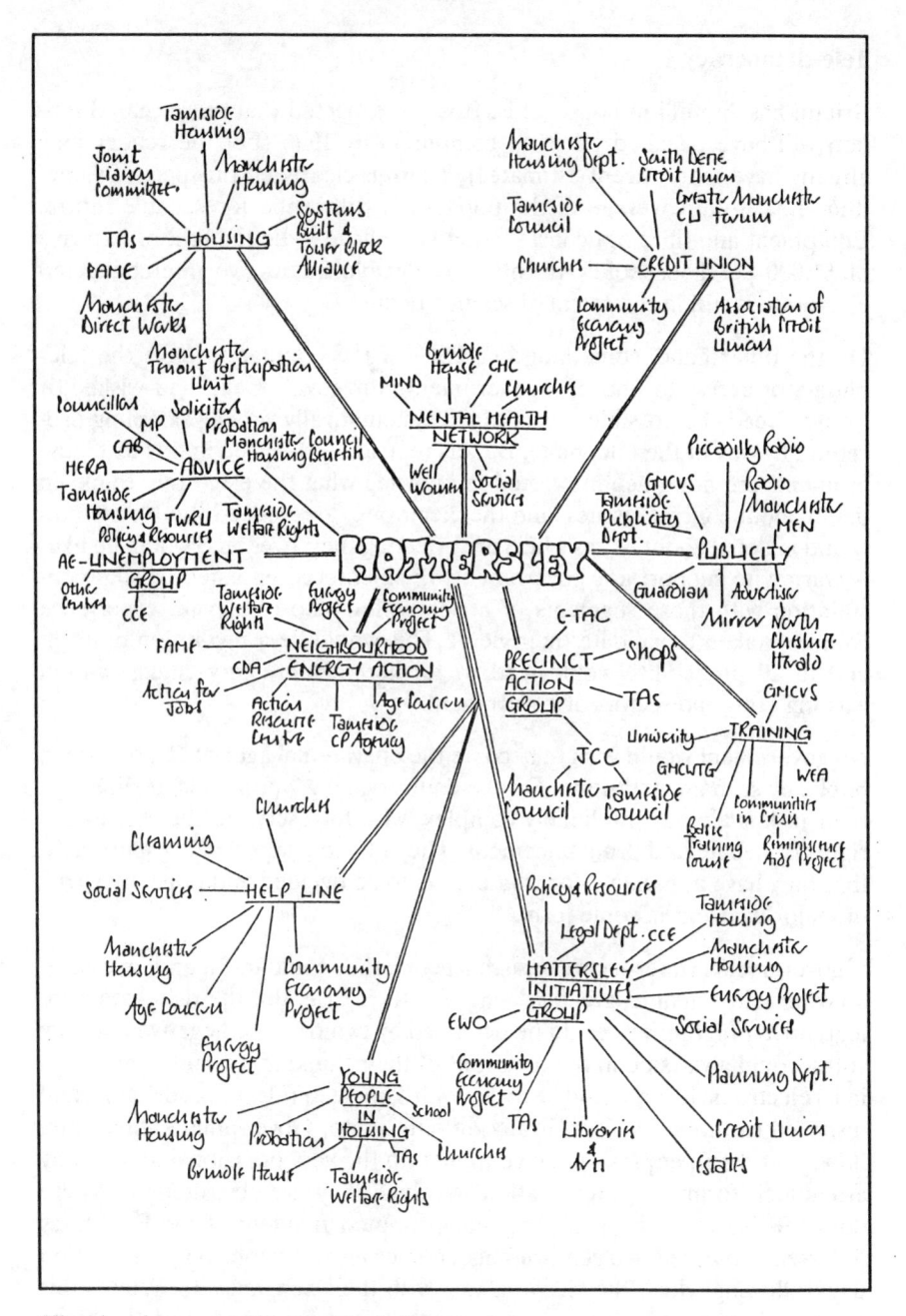

The development of networks in Hattersley

Tele-democracy

Britain has 22 million households. It is not expected that more than 3 million will have installed personal computers by 1996 (but the reader may already have more recent estimates). There is clearly no prospect of something near total coverage of the population within the foreseeable future. Equipment and fibre optic installation costs have to be thought of in terms of £1,000 per household. An infinitely flexible interactive interconnected electorate is still in the realm of science fiction.

On the other hand, something like 95% of the population have the telephone, or access to one. If a government, any government, had wished, it would already be possible to institute a systematically varying sampling procedure by way of the telephone. But, as repeatedly asserted in this text, governments are not much interested in knowing what the electorate thinks in detail about concrete issues: and the electorate does indeed think concretely and in detail about issues which are affecting their lives, and would be likely warmly to support any government which entered into step-by-step consultation with those segments of a population whose relevant experience could be taken to validate their views. This would be a revolution in itself, and in all probability would lead to further revolutionary change within existing arms and sectors of government.

No government would wish to become the operational agency of a sovereign public by such an institution. On the contrary, all governments, feeling that their task is already intolerably complex, wish to reserve to themselves the rights of debate and pronouncement. They like to claim, usually spuriously, that they have a mandate for whatever is to be decided and done, by virtue of majority assent in some form.

If governments were sincere in such a claim, they could test it and, in case of a favourable outcome, greatly strengthen their case. But the risk that entire legislative programmes could be de-railed by two or three negative majority votes would always be in the forefront of their thinking. Instant democracy, in its electronic form, would be an awkward horse to ride, unpredictable, and disposed to throw its rider at any difficult jump. Governments, therefore, hope that their peoples will be content with the very occasional and greatly attenuated form of representation to which they are accustomed. Where does this leave the people? The much-vaunted freedom of the British, as Rousseau observed two centuries ago, comes into existence only on election day, following which they have to live with their new masters. Why is this spectral form of democracy still accepted? One is reminded of the acute Irish observation: *"Get a name for an early riser and you can lie in bed 'til noon."* This conclusion is very much in line with the anarchist stance.

Are we, therefore, to press for some form of electronic teledemocracy? This would be a discouraging task when one considers the glacial slowness of progression towards so slight a change as that entailed by proportional representation. Michael Rustin has written:

> *Similarly, better technical resources may make it possible to operate an income maintenance or combined tax/benefit system that is more flexibly, transparently and speedily adjusted to meet differentiated needs — for example, those of single parents or the low paid. The customization of personal insurance and pensions by the private financial sector is an example of what new technologies might have made possible for the public sector in this sphere. One could similarly imagine a public housing system in which allocation, transfer and choice would be made much more competitive with private ownership, through the use of appropriate information systems. One can also conceive of new interactive technologies being used in support of public access to information, and to make involvement in the political process more direct and easy. Participation in neighbourhood council school governors, or even internal party elections could be made much less onerous if votes were cast through computer terminals linked into urban or national fibre-optic cable networks. Technological developments favouring customization, and the culture which emerges from their diffusion in the market sector, undoubtedly change both the environment of provision and choice and people's expectations of services. There are good reasons for thinking about how the provisions of the public domain could be improved by such technical means.* (New Left Review 175, 1989.)

This takes us far beyond the simplicities of tele-voting. It conceives of interactive networks at local, administrative and governmental levels. It sees the possibility of direct public access to information.It could lead into areas of public administration, involving an immense range of computer-stored detail. One's medical history, educational record, tax liability, welfare entitlement and credit rating could be summoned to appear on one's T.V. screen, as are the weather, road reports and cricket scores by Ceefax/Oracle. What is made available to us at the moment is whatever is politically expedient for governments. There would be security problems in any such development. Some Personal Identification Number system would be required. This becomes a technical problem, capable of resolution. The importance of access to detailed information, not only relating to the individual but to community, employment, social statistics, local and national, cannot be over-stressed. By contrast, the prospect of a mass society voting on a basis of slanted and false information, unceasingly propagated by the media moguls, does not bear contemplation.

It must be emphasised that teledemocracy is not conceived as a quick move towards endless national referenda. Most issues will be local or sectoral. There is much to be said for Burnheim's principle that only those whose material interests are involved should be eligible to record their opinions. Something more like a grounded system is envisaged, generating a constant circulation and re-circulation of proposals and preferences. The melt-down of perspectives and experiences should lead towards a crystallisation. This will often reveal a positive/negative polarisation, which in turn will call for further resolution.

The Personal Ethic

The contemporary world is awash with vast sums of money, often in the form of liquid finance capital, ceaselessly seeking out opportunities for safe and lucrative investment. The global economic system is, however, precariously poised, most countries being exposed as debtors or creditors to the uncertain outcomes of international debts of unthinkable proportions, and to balance of payments problems which may be insoluble. The system may collapse, or go into deep recession. Meanwhile, the Nikkei, Dow Jones and F.E. 100 indices on the world's stock exchanges show a continuing, if uneven, upward gradient. Their apparent strength is not closely related to production and exchange, nor to the material realities therefore, but rather reflects the necessity for the great financial corporations to find some kind of lodgment for the funds they manage. These developments are of vast consequence for the world including the exploited third world, by way of international trading.

A general effect has been a sharpening of ethical issues, among which we distinguish three, none of them new, but all of increasing salience.

First, there is a great increase in the scale of corruption. Sums as large as fifty million pounds for a single individual have been mentioned as payment for the procurement of an arms contract. Industrial consortia learn how to lose their slush fund in the general accounts. In some countries, corruption has become so rife that an air ticket is hardly procurable without financial inducement to the booking clerk. In third world countries where an exemplary life-style exhibiting all the virtues of moderation, may have been adopted, by a leader such as Julius Nyerere, Robert Mugabe or Mahatma

Gandhi before them, elite business chiefs, bankers or civil servants have commonly chosen the primrose path. Luxury, high living and capital accumulation proliferate, amongst absolute destitution evident on the pavement outside, as in nineteenth century London. It may be that, in building for themselves a life of pleasure and privilege in the present, while loyally bestowing favours on relatives and exacting tribute from dependent strangers, they were behaving in accordance with their traditional culture. Payment for favours, a corrupt practice in the view of a liberal capitalist ethic, might seem to them normal, an exchange system that maintains the whole social structure. Such attitudes may unfit them for responsibilities in a western-type, depersonalised, legal-rational bureaucracy: but not everyone considers bureaucracy so necessary, or even ethically admirable, as we have all been led to suppose. Max Weber explored this issue with great mastery.

The second issue is that which concerns application of vast quantities of surplus finance capital to social ends. No-one credits the long out-dated claims of the laissez faire school, that capital yields maximum social returns when competing for maximum profit. Most wealthy people speak publicly in such terms but the ghastly social consequences of basing government policies on such a belief, in the U.S.A. specifically, but in Britain also, through the 1980s, stand in flat contradiction of any such simple faith. We may say that everyone knows that to be the case: the doubts that an electorate might have on the alternatives to that faith however, are realistic enough.

In either case, the questions surrounding the allocation of capital resources demand answers. Large churches, such as the Church of England, may find themselves in possession of urban slum property, from which they derive a large income. They may discover that the huge sums managed for them on the advice of honourable but sometimes mistaken, investment experts, are drawing large returns from South African gold mines and the sale of armaments to Arab countries. The churches are putting their houses in order by re-distributing their investments, as are some universities. The effect of course is to leave lucrative sectors of the economy to those without such scruples.

Third is the range of issues in the sphere of personal ethics. It is striking that so little ethical advice relating to the world of work is on offer from the churches or political parties. One hardly expects it from trades unions or employers. It seems that the need to find work and to gain the material comforts that are derived from it are seen not merely as paramount, but as absolute. Such questions as: Is your occupation of value to the community? How might it affect you if you stay with it for several years? How might it affect your family, and the lives of your family? -seem not to be discussed very much at interview. Perhaps the best employment counsellors do raise them with their clients but the main focus appears to be on qualifications and aptitude. The relative absence of such issues in career advice and in Further Education is deplorable — the more so because the client/applicant will normally be found responsive to them; even seeking answers to such questions.

These issues are central to the "quality of life" — in quotes because the concept is gathering status in such socio-medical fields as geriatrics, the management of terminal illness, job satisfaction, stress and its psycho-somatic derivatives.

On all the above ethical issues, co-operatives win hands down. Because of the openness of all of their proceedings and the possibilities of face-to-face challenge, they have a transparency in sharp contrast to the opacity of both private and bureaucratic systems. The anxiety level is reduced. That opacity, often intentional, is the source of much disenchantment and disincentive among workers. The conversation of workers everywhere is rich in colourful and cynical reference to the obscurities, irrationalities and inequities of decisions at higher levels. Systems may be described as "Kafka-esque" when discussions affecting everyone are held behind closed doors, even in quite small enterprises. In that climate, self-interest and corruption can flourish; it appears that even qualified and professional accountants are willing to certify mystificatory statements that do not reveal the distribution of benefits. Such machinations would not survive a week in a genuine co-operative system. Workers would know that the organisation is honest, because it is theirs and is open to challenge at all points. This is probably the greatest single determinant of good morale and of commitment.

One cannot be so confident about other ethical issues. A young person who wishes to make money quickly will not choose the co-operative path. He/she will not choose honourable employment in local government, social services or education. Nor will the choice fall on the production of goods, even on a large scale; nor the shabby world of parliament. By one route or another, they will be attracted towards the financial world — the merchant banks the currency dealers, the investment advisers, the accountants, the company lawyers, the take-over specialists, who may put together, break up or sell off the firms to which others have given their working lives. To achieve 20% surplus on the £50,000 turn-over of a co-operative would not interest them. They would be looking for 1/4% for themselves on a transaction involving £50 million — arranged for their clients and requiring no more than a few weeks' work. The possibly more ethical co-operator may see his former school-friend already wealthy for less effort, it may be. A co-operator's wife raising young children, may be even more aware of the discrepancy. Personal insurance and pension rights may still further sharpen their perceptions.

If the comparison were to be phrased in terms of quality of life, however, a different balance might be struck. Who is more at risk from heart disease; alcoholism; stress conditions? What are the relative indices of family problems? What degrees of job satisfaction are reported? If the very real benefits of the co-operative way of life are to be achieved, however, a commitment to it must be maintained through good years and bad, a commitment not too dependent on annual returns, though certainly taking them very much into account. When the calculation has been made, the ultimate choice to be made is an ethical one.

Terminal Questions

Among the questions which motivated this over-view of self-management were the following:

Have unsupported self-managing enterprises proved their viability over time?

Yes; beyond question.

Are they a real alternative to free capitalism, on the one hand, and socialist nationalisation on the other?

Yes; they seem capable of functioning within a variety of systems.

Can industrial co-operatives become socially responsible for external effects of their operation, as private enterprise never has?

This is problematic; but they are socially aware, and more responsible than private firms.

Can they offer a social philosophy with a form of government?

Not yet: but it is conceivable that they might generate one.

Why have co-operatives achieved so little in third world development?

In the third world, social development is extinguished in favour of highly capitalised enterprise, local privilege and land-ownership.

Will we not see the same process of extinction in Western economies as co-operatives become larger and more successful?

This is only too probable.

It is frustrating that this text, reduced from an original double its present length, has had to present its evidence in a form so truncated as to disrupt the coherence of the intended argument.

Perhaps the reader will be willing to allow for this, and consider the central propositions concerning feasibility, range, quality of life and the learning that self-government entails. Also the historical observation that it is vulnerable to pressures from within the free-enterprises economics which do not wish to see it succeed, from their governments and the unfavourable legislation which they impose upon it. And finally that there is infinite scope for realistic development and sophisticated presentation of its claims. It has not been by-passed by the development of capitalism. Every generation has demonstrated that what it has to offer is an enormous range of possibilities of the greatest value.

Bibliography

Hundreds of sources have been consulted in preparing the fore-going text. Many have been ephemeral; the following lists include selected pamphlet material, in addition to books.

Kibbutz

Kibbutz in the Market Society, Stanley Maron. Israel 1993

International Communal Studies Association. Bulletin nos 7, 8, 10—13.

Israel 1990 — 93.

Kibbutz Trends, nos 7, 9, and 10. Israel 1992 — 3.

Kibbutz Studies, nos 32/33. Israel 1990.

Athens

In classical studies the most up-to-date studies are not always the most valid.

Browning, R. (Ed). The Greeks. New York, 1985.

Castle, E.B. Ancient Education. London, 1961.

Farrington, B. Greek Science. London, 1944.

Ferguson, F. and Chisholm, K. Political and Social Life in the Great Age of Athens. Milton Keynes, 1978.

Finley, M.I. Democracy Ancient and Modern. London, 1985.

Forbes, R.J. and Dijksterhuis, E.J. A History of Science and Technology, Vol. I. London, 1963.

Green, P. Concise History of Ancient Greece, London, 1974.

Hutten, E. The Origins of Science, London, 1962.

Kitto, H.D.F. The Greeks, London, 1952.

Ling, R. Classical Greece. Oxford, 1988.

Stone, I. F. The Trial of Socrates. London, 1989.

Werner, P. Life in Greece in Ancient Times. Geneva, 1978.

Quakers

Hubbard, G. Quaker by Convincement. London

Fryer, J. George Fox and the Children of Light, London, 1991.

Cockcroft, J. et al. Questions of Integrity; a Quaker Perspective. London, 1993.

Sheeran, M.J. Beyond Majority Rule. Philadelphia, 1983.

Windsor, D.B. The Quaker Enterprise. London, 1980.

Booklets from Friends House, London:

Sharman, C. Servant of the Meeting, 1983.

Wilsher, B. Quaker Organisation, 1986.

Self-Government in Industry

Oakeshott, R. The Case for Workers' Co-ops. London, 1978.

Oakeshott, R. with Wiener, H. Worker-Owners. Mondragon Revisited.

Anglo-German Foundation for the Study of Industrial Society, London, 1987.

Spear, R. Bibliography of Worker Coop Publications. Co-operative Research Unit, the Open University, Milton Keynes, 1990.

The following are research reports or papers of some substance.

Dharam Ghai. Participatory Development. U.N. Research Institute for Social Development. Geneva.

Stern, E. Worker Co-operatives in France, Italy and the U.K. Tavistock Institute, and H.M.S.O.

Bartlett,W. and Pridham, G. Co-operative Enterprises in Italy, Portugal and Spain. S.A.U.S. and Evolution of Workers' Co-operative in Southern Europe, S.A.U.S. University of Bristol.

Cornford, J.A. Stake in the Company: E.S.O.P.'s. Institute for Public Policy Research, London, 1990.

Anon. No Single Model. Institute for Common Ownership. Leeds, 1986.

Anon. Seikatsu Club Consumer's Co-operative. Tokyo, 1993.

Annual Reports of the National Freight Corporation; The John Lewis Partnership; Scott Bader; The Co-operative Retail Service and the C.W.S.; the Co-operative Bank; Industrial Common Ownership Finance.

Leaderless Groups

Bion, W.R. Experiences in Groups. London, 1961.

Foulkes, S.H. and Anthony, E.J. Group Psychotherapy, London, 1965.

Freud, S. Group Psychology and the Analysis of the Ego. London, 1955.

Lewin, K. Field Theory in Social Science. New York, 1951.

Nichol, J.B. Early Development of Group Psychotherapy in Britain. Occasional Paper, School of Education, Manchester University.

Anarchism

Kropotkin, P. Mutual Aid. London, 1902.

Kropotkin, P. Fields, Factories and Workshops Tomorrow. London, 1974.

Miller, D. Anarchism. London, 1984.

Rocker, R. Anarcho-Syndicalism. London, 1989.

Woodcock, G. The Anarchist Reader. London, 1977.

Education and the Quality of Life

Zadek, S. and Evans, R. Auditing the Market. Traidcraft. Gateshead, 1993.

Tolstoy, L. The School at Yasnaya Polyana. Intro Archambault, R.D., tr. Wiener, L., in Tolstoy on Education. Chicago, 1967.

Neill, A.S. Summerhill. London, 1962.

Fletcher, C. The Challenges of Community Education. University of Nottingham, 1984.

Ireland, T.D. Gelpi's View of Lifelong Education. Manchester, 1978.

Democracy (Chapters 1 and 10)

Held, D. Political Theory and the Modern State. Cambridge, 1989.

Keane, J. The Media and Democracy. Cambridge, 1991.

de Tocqueville, A. Democracy in America. Paris, 1835.

Resources and Teaching Aids. The Politics Association, Manchester, 1993/4.

Illich, I. et al. Disabling Professions. London, 1977.

Bestuzhev-Lada, I. In the Contemporary Review No. 1505, 1991.

Frey, J.G. Survey Research by Telephone. Sage, 1983.

Some Items on Self-Management

The New Internationalist is a monthly journal focusing on issues of world poverty and injustice between nations. It formed itself into a co-operative of fourteen partners. Each number is edited by a different member, in turn. This valuable initiative, setting itself against the prevailing commercial ethos, has a record of steady and increasing success. Its circulation has reached 50,000; there are offices in Canada, the U.S.A., New Zealand and Australia, as well as its home base in the U.K. Of recent years, a stream of papers and booklets on co-operatives has become available from Ken Coates at the Institute for Workers' Control, originally funded by Bertrand Russell; from the Co-operative Research Unit at the Open University, notably from the hand of Chris Cornforth; and from the Industrial Common Ownership Movement, with several contributors. Their addresses are as follows:

I.W.C. and Spokesman Books, Bertrand Russell House, Gamble St., Nottingham, NG7 4ET.

C.R.U. Technology Faculty, Open University, Walton Hall, Milton Keynes, Buckinghamshire.

I.C.O.M., 7/8, Corn Exchange, Leeds, LS1 7BP.